DAY TRADING
ATTENTION

DAY TRADING ATTENTION

HOW TO ACTUALLY BUILD BRAND AND SALES IN THE NEW SOCIAL MEDIA WORLD

GARY VAYNERCHUK

HARPER
BUSINESS

An Imprint of HarperCollinsPublishers

HarperCollins books may be purchased for educational, business, or sales promotional use. For information, please email the Special Markets Department at SPsales@harpercollins.com.

First HarperBusiness hardcover published 2024

FIRST EDITION

Designed by Nancy Singer

Library of Congress Cataloging-in-Publication Data has been applied for.

ISBN 978-0-06-331759-8

24 25 26 27 28 LBC 5 4 3 2 1

This book is dedicated to the 1 percent that make consumer-centric decisions vs the 99 percent that make decisions based on boardroom politics.

CONTENTS

AUTHOR'S NOTE

The feedback I'll provide on various pieces of content in this book are the opinions of myself and my team, based on our experience. I cannot claim any knowledge of any business's agenda or original intent. I'm just using it as an opportunity to paint a clearer picture for all of you.

INTRODUCTION

Nathan Apodaca unintentionally made one of the greatest modern advertisements.

Nathan, known as "Doggface" on the internet, was a regular guy working at a potato factory in Idaho when he decided to take his longboard to work one day. As he was cruising down the side of the road on his way to the factory, he pulled out his phone and filmed himself on the front-facing camera. He recorded a short video of himself enjoying the vibes—just lip-syncing the lyrics to a Fleetwood Mac song that he had playing in the background and taking a sip out of his jug of Ocean Spray cran-raspberry juice.

Nathan didn't think much of it. Eventually, right before he got into work, he casually posted the clip on TikTok.

Later that day, he was stunned to see that video had over 2 million views.

It continued to go viral and amassed millions more views (around 90 million views at the time of writing). Soon after, Nathan's whole life changed. He started getting approached by brands for sponsorship deals. He got interviewed by major media outlets. He later released a song with Snoop Dogg and had an acting debut in a television show. At the time of writing, he has 7.5 million followers on TikTok, 2.5 million followers on Instagram, and 276,000 subscribers on YouTube.

The video also dramatically impacted Ocean Spray's business. The content made the brand relevant not only to the younger audience that you might think is the platform's core demographic, but also to the thirty-, forty-, and fifty-year-olds who consume TikTok at scale today. Their juice was flying off the shelves at retail locations across the US.

That's not all. The song "Dreams" by Fleetwood Mac (which was playing in the background of the video) hit the top of the iTunes charts, even though the song itself was originally released in 1977.

The craziest part?

Nathan almost didn't even post the video. He said in an interview with *Big Boy's Neighborhood*, "I was like, 'Man, maybe I shouldn't post it' . . . I looked at it again, and I was like, 'Okay, remember what GaryVee says all the time: Post out content, let it get out there. It doesn't matter if I don't think it's good. Somebody out there wants to see me.'"[1]

This Ocean Spray story is just one of many examples that capture what modern advertising looks like. There are countless brands, small businesses, service providers, influencers, and content creators that have seen life-changing sales numbers from content that didn't look like traditional "commercials" or banner ads. For instance, a hip-hop themed lip balm brand named TrapStix had 75 orders between 2018 and 2020. After a series of overperforming Tik-

Tok videos, they went on to sell 50,000 units in two years.[2] Similarly, a daughter helped turn her dad's novel into a bestseller more than a decade after its release, thanks to a popular video she made.[3] Stories like these are happening around the world every day.

It's not just TikTok either. Small businesses are using YouTube Shorts to rank their videos in search queries to drive leads. Plenty of creators across YouTube, TikTok, Facebook, Snapchat, Instagram, LinkedIn, and X (Twitter) are using these platforms to build massive communities of their own, and even create their own products that rival those of larger brands. As I'm writing this, my team and I are using Facebook Reels to drive sign-ups for WineText.com, a deal-of-the-day wine SMS service associated with my dad's business. (By the way, if you just signed up at WineText.com, please email my dad at sasha@winelibrary.com. He would love to hear from you, and I know that this would make his day, his week, his month, and his year, which would be the biggest return on investment of this book.)

If you picked up this book, you probably already know you should be on social media. Compared to October 2009, when my first book, *Crush It!*, came out, there are far fewer people who doubt that social media "works." However, only a small percentage of that group truly understands how to use modern advertising platforms to build brand and grow sales in today's rapidly changing environment.

This book will give you the blueprint.

Day Trading Attention (and Why It Matters)

In 2013, I wrote *Jab, Jab, Jab, Right Hook: How to Tell Your Story in a Noisy Social World*. It was a guide on how to communicate on the social platforms of the day. Given how much the advertising landscape has changed in the ten years that have since passed, I figured it was time for an updated version.

I thought about calling this book *Jab, Jab, Jab, Left Hook*, a fitting name for a sequel. I eventually decided on *Day Trading Attention* because it best describes not only what I do for a living, but also the number one skill set that you need to master in today's advertising landscape: understanding attention— what it is, where it is, where it's underpriced, and how to leverage it for brand building and sales.

This isn't a book about *just* social media—it's a book about mastering the art and science of storytelling in modern underpriced attention channels. Of course, social media happens to be a huge part of that, but as you'll see over the course of this book, it can also involve strategies like event marketing, developing collectible products, running ads on streaming services, brand collaborations, influencer partnerships, and potentially even traditional advertising campaigns like TV commercials or billboards in some cases.

Just as a day trader constantly studies financial markets to keep a pulse on what's happening, you must constantly study what people are paying attention to, the cost associated with capturing that attention, and how it shifts by the day. This is how you'll find the best marketing and sales strategies for your business or brand. Think of it this way: If you know *what* people are paying attention to and *where* they're paying attention, then you actually have a shot at selling them something.

This is what marketers have been doing for generations: identifying where human attention lies and reverse-engineering it. For instance, the radio gets invented, people start listening to it, and marketers realize, *Hey, I can pay money to the radio station so they'll let me pop in while people are listening, and I can sell them my stuff. This radio station talks about baseball, and people listening are probably baseball fans, so why don't I tie some baseball references into my script, so they'll be more interested in listening to me?*

Same thing with television. The TV is invented, shows are created, and people start watching, and marketers realize, *Hey, I can show up while people are watching and show them why my company has the best laundry detergent ever.*

You can even take this concept back to the Stone Age. I bet if somebody wanted to sell you a new club, they would draw on the cave walls because that's where all the cavemen were most likely to look.

Attention is the game. More specifically, *underpriced* attention is the opportunity.

To understand what that means, think of attention as an asset. It's like buying real estate. Fifty years ago, if you believed that Malibu was going to grow in popularity and home prices would go up, you would've first studied all the tactical nuances of buying beachfront property in that area, and then you would've bought as much as you possibly could before prices started rising even further. Similarly, when an advertising platform has a lot of eyes and ears on it, and the cost of storytelling on that platform is relatively low, that's when you need to go all in. Just like certain cities have underpriced real estate, certain advertising platforms have underpriced attention.

That being said, underpriced attention isn't just about what advertising medium is the cheapest; it's about whether you can get a low cost *relative* to the amount of actual attention you'd get.

Let me explain.

In the 1950s, one of the mediums with underpriced consumer attention happened to be television. According to some estimates, 90 percent of American households had a television set by 1960, and unlike today, people actually watched TV commercials back then. Some brands realized this early on, and aggressively launched TV strategies with mascots, taglines, and catchy jingles. In the 1950s, brands were also able to have creative control over producing shows on TV, which led to programs like *Hallmark Hall of Fame* and *The Colgate Comedy Hour*. Roy Disney (Walt Disney's older brother) even made a catchy jingle out of the slogan "I Like Ike," which was then run as TV commercials, eventually contributing to Dwight D. Eisenhower winning the 1952 presidential election. The proof was clearly there—television held a vast majority of underpriced consumer attention.

As the years passed and technology began to evolve, however, the attention shifted.

The number of consumers watching traditional cable television today is dramatically declining. The 2022 coverage of the Winter Olympics drew the lowest ratings in the event's history on NBC.[4] According to some studies, top cable providers had a net loss of 3.5 million video subscribers in 2022.[5] With other mediums like social media and streaming platforms creating more competition for consumer attention, advertising on television just isn't what it used to be in the 1950s, '60s, '70s, or '80s. But still, the cost of TV commercials is upward of $100,000 in many cases; the price hasn't adjusted much for the decline in attention over the years.[6]

What does this mean? While television commercials can still "work," they are generally overpriced. Sure, if you're spending over $100,000 on a commercial, you're going to sell some stuff. But what if you allocated that same $100,000 on a well-executed, modern advertising strategy grounded in social media? Would you sell even more? More interestingly, could you extract insights from your social media campaigns to help you make even better commercials (should you still decide to run them)?

By no means am I telling brands to never run another television ad again. In fact, even though traditional television commercials are overpriced as a whole, there is one major exception: Super Bowl commercials. I believe the Super Bowl commercial is the single greatest deal in advertising in the US, even at $7 million for a thirty-second spot as I'm writing this in 2023.[7] One hundred fifteen million people watched the most recent Super Bowl in the United States, and it's a part of the culture for Americans to sit down and watch those ads too. That level of consumption is impossible to replicate with even the best social media strategies. Believe it or not, I think Super Bowl commercials are a bargain; they can really work for brands, assuming the ad is good (we'll get into that later). Similarly, regular TV commercials can occasionally work, if the ad was bought in a very strategic way and the creative was remarkable and well priced.

The issue is, most of today's television commercials and other traditional marketing executions are not Super Bowl ads, nor are they purchased at an appropriate price—so, why do so many marketers, brands, and corporations still treat them like religion? It's because people tend to dismiss what's underpriced today, and instead focus on what used to work in the past, or what might work in the future. In the process, they continue to underestimate what's working right now.

It's why some small business owners and professionals still say, "TikTok can't generate leads like SEO," or "LinkedIn doesn't convert as well as Google AdWords." In the 1950s, those same people would've said, "Television commercials don't work as well as radio ads"—and they would've been wrong. In the early 2000s, those people would've said that Google Ads were a waste of time. In the

mid-1990s, when I was running my dad's liquor store, those people told me that having a website was stupid and that I should just open up another store for Wine Library. In the late '90s, they told me email wouldn't replace catalogs.

I get it. People always have reactions like these when new technology comes along and changes the way we do things. Still, I wish more businesses and brands understood that they're only hurting themselves. By continuing to underestimate modern advertising platforms, they're leaving ridiculous amounts of opportunity on the table, and they don't have to.

Let me ask you, marketers and executives: Why are you always a "no" person in the face of new opportunities? Why can't you be a "maybe" person, do your homework, and then decide if it's a "yes" or "no"?

Many fast-growing brands today have been built on the back of smart modern advertising executions—companies like True Classic and Fashion Nova to name a couple, not to mention companies built around personal brands such as Chamberlain Coffee (founded by popular YouTuber and content creator Emma

Chamberlain). I built Wine Library primarily by using underpriced mediums in the 1990s and early 2000s: Google AdWords, email marketing, and organic YouTube videos.

Day trading underpriced attention is what has historically worked best in advertising.

What does this mean for you? For large companies and brands, it's time to think beyond the "potential reach" that TV commercials, print ads, billboards, or digital programmatic banner ads offer. For small business owners and professionals, it's time to expand beyond the old, traditional sales strategies of Google AdWords, SEO, SEM, cold calling, referrals, or going to the chamber of commerce. For creators and influencers, it's time to get more strategic about the content you're putting out instead of posting just to post and expand the platforms you're posting on.

I'm not saying you should entirely stop cold-calling or whatever is working for you right now. I don't like to think of any marketing or sales method as "dead." I just think there's a much smarter way to build a modern, cohesive advertising strategy, one that has social media at the core and uses insights from social campaigns to inform all the other pieces. In fact, I can't wait to make fun of people who are overinvesting in social media in a decade or two.

Today, mass consumer attention sits across a handful of social media platforms, which happen to have literally zero cost for organic reach (the number of people who will see your content if you just post it, without running it as an ad). That's why social media can be one of the best places to capture underpriced attention. For example, Facebook has an estimated 3 billion monthly active users at the time of writing.[8] Instagram and YouTube each have roughly over 2 billion, and LinkedIn has 930 million members.[9] [10] [11]

Influencers promoting your product or service can also be an underpriced strategy, assuming you choose up-and-coming influencers who are relatively low cost. Same applies to event marketing, ads on streaming services, brand collaborations, developing collectible items related to your business, and all the other opportunities I'll talk about in this book.

But here's the catch: Even if you're on social media—even if you are running ads on Hulu instead of a cable TV network—it doesn't mean it'll work for you. You actually have to be good at the execution.

As soon as I sensed that people were paying attention to TikTok, I knew I needed to figure out all the tactics and details of how to storytell within that platform. I needed to figure out how to make videos people want to watch, how to use different creative units (that is, carousels versus stand-alone images versus videos), what the first few seconds of my videos should look like, what trending audio I should use in the background, how to decide when to duet or stitch a video, and more.

Social media is just an empty vessel; you only get out of it what you put into it. Without putting in the work to understand these platforms and the psychology of the people using them, you're just creating a bunch of content that no one will ever see. If you make videos for Tik-Tok that no one wants to watch or spend

$10,000 running Facebook ads with content that doesn't captivate people, then social media will be a "waste of time and money." If you overpay for influencer endorsements that don't lead to sales, then influencer marketing will be a "waste of time and money." It's like how playing basketball could earn you a lot of money in theory, but you have to be a good basketball player to actually achieve that. Just because you're marketing on social media doesn't mean you're good at it. If you're not good at it, it may not work for you.

It's important to recognize what advertising mediums are traditionally overpriced versus underpriced, but it's also important to know how to make them work for you, given the resources you have available.

That's what you'll learn in this book. With the in-depth strategies, frameworks, and tactics in the coming pages, you'll be better equipped than most to advertise (and grow) your business or brand in the world that we currently live in.

The New Social Media World

Back when I wrote *Jab, Jab, Jab, Right Hook*, I defined the concept as "give, give,

give, ask." In other words, make content that gives value to your audience so that you have permission to "ask" for their business down the road. The "jabs" (free value) would set up the "right hook" (the ask) in the algorithm—with how various social platforms worked back then, getting high engagement on one of your posts meant that future posts would be more likely to be shown to those individuals who engaged. So, it made sense to create a "jab" that engaged a wider audience so that more people would see and engage with your right hook. Providing free value was also just a good way to build trust and affinity with your audience so they'd be more receptive to things you ask for down the road.

Over the last decade, algorithms across platforms have evolved dramatically. Today, there are far more variables to consider when producing content.

For example, what should "free value" look like now? What should the layout, design, and formatting look like? How do you decide what pieces of content to make, and how can you create a process to make that production sustainable? How should your content change depending on the platform you're posting on? Could a piece of content that builds brand also drive sales at the same time? How can content like Doggface's Ocean

Spray video drive so many sales, when it doesn't even look like a "right hook"?

As we think about these answers, let's take a step back for a second and start from the most basic advertising question of all: What's the reason that human beings buy certain products and services instead of others? Whether it's through social media or anywhere else—what *actually* gets someone to buy that latest business software tool, or their newest T-shirt, or the watch they're wearing?

Sometimes it's because the product was at a convenient location, they were able to get it at a cheap price, or maybe a friend recommended it to them. But you'd be surprised how often people subconsciously buy things because the brand or business *means* something to them. In other words, they decide that a certain product or service is more *relevant* to their needs or to who they are. That is the power of "brand" at work.

For example, maybe an accountant got you to trust his or her expertise by posting thoughtful information about taxes online. Maybe a sneaker brand collaborated with your favorite athlete, and that made you buy. Maybe a skincare brand made a funny reference to a Netflix series you like, and the next time you were in the mall or drugstore, you picked up their product because you subconsciously felt "closer" to that brand than their competitors. Maybe a couple of law firm partners created an entertaining podcast about golf, an area you're passionate about, and the next time you had a business contract to get done, you thought of them first. Maybe a B2B company created smart content on how their software would save you money, and that made you buy. Many of our purchasing decisions are influenced by how we consciously—or subconsciously—feel about a brand. I'll buy virtually anything if the ad has a positive New York Jets reference tied into it ;).

What this means is that content alone is not enough; content that scales brand relevance is the goal. Relevance is defined as "a close connection with the subject you are discussing or the situation you are in."[12] We need to tell stories that help people feel closely connected to our businesses and brands.

It's not just about letting consumers know your business or your brand exists. It's not about posting random content just for the sake of posting it. If you're a florist, for example, you can't just post a picture of a flower with "happy Tuesday" in the caption and call it a day. Relevance is about creating and distributing content that people find meaningful (whether that's potential customers, clients, or other individuals who matter to you). When your business is more relevant, more people consider buying, which then leads to higher sales numbers.

Why did Doggface's Ocean Spray video drive sales? It made the brand more relevant to a variety of different demographics. Whether intentional or not, there was something about the video that struck a chord with people—maybe it was the camera angle, maybe it was the length of the video that made it easily consumable, maybe it was the vibe of the song that was added to the video, maybe it was the style of movement in the first few seconds, maybe it was the lighthearted nature of someone just enjoying life, or maybe it was a combination of all of these elements and more. The strategy behind how you make your content (such as, what your first three seconds look like) and your understanding of platform nuances (such as, what trending audio to use on TikTok versus Instagram) are two of many tools you can use to make content that's more relevant.

One of the biggest changes in the new

social media world is that the more relevant your content is to an audience, the more your content will be distributed by the platform itself. As I'll talk about more in part 1 of this book, all platforms are heading in the direction of showing content to users based on what they're interested in, rather than who they follow. The more relevant your content is to an audience, the more they will be interested in consuming it, and the more reach you'll get.

This means that the quality of the content that you put out is more important than ever. I don't mean production quality, or whether you subjectively like the piece of content or not—I mean, are you putting out stuff that a group of people is interested in consuming?

For content to be relevant and drive business results, it needs to be more strategic and thoughtful than ever before. You need to consider variables like:

- What time are you posting?
- What title do you have as a text overlay on your video?
- Who are you making your piece of content for? Why should they be interested in consuming it?

- If you post a video on TikTok, how are you tweaking it before you post on, say, YouTube Shorts?
- Is your post caption (aka copy) optimized?
- What creative units are you using? (Creative units are different content creation features on platforms, like stories, carousels, Reels on Instagram, or status updates on Facebook.)
- What creative styles are you using? (Meaning, ways of displaying content within creative units, such as a skit on Instagram Reel.)
- How are you deciding what piece of content to run as a paid ad?
- Are your profiles on each platform optimized correctly so people know what you do, and how to contact you?
- How can you use insights from social media content to inform larger advertising strategies, such as trade shows, TV commercials, or higher-production videos?

And much, much, much, much more.

These are the kinds of concepts we'll explore in depth in this book.

The Supply and Demand of Content (and Why You Need to Act Now)

The opportunity is enormous for everyone reading this—as more platforms are distributing content based on what people are interested in rather than who they follow, it's more practical than ever for creators, businesses, and brands alike to achieve more relevance and grow. Even if they don't have an audience. But the reality is, the opportunities on platforms today won't last forever.

Why? It's a concept I call the Supply and Demand of Content.

When there's a lot of attention on a platform (especially when it's early in its maturity), you have a greater chance to get awareness and engagement on your content because there aren't as many content producers and advertisers on the platform yet. As a platform gets more and more mature, it gets harder to have your content stand out.

Between mid-2021 and 2022, my You-Tube channel saw some of the greatest spikes in views that I've ever received, largely thanks to the disproportionately high organic reach of YouTube Shorts when they were first released to the public in July 2021. At that point, there were fewer content creators on YouTube Shorts compared to the number of people who wanted to watch that type of content. Today, YouTube Shorts is still a huge opportunity for many brands and business owners. YouTube is the second-biggest search engine in the world, so posting Shorts and long-form videos with search-engine-optimized titles can help increase the discoverability of your content. However, as more time passes, the more strategy and thoughtfulness it will take to stand out.

The Supply and Demand of Content applies to features and content formats within platforms too.

For example, in 2015 and 2016, I was getting dozens of emails a day from people saying they made the biggest business development deals of their lives through Instagram direct message (DM). At that point, some celebrities and executives were more directly reachable through their DMs than other forms of contact, so reaching out to them with an offer to bring value was more likely to get you a response. It's the same reason email marketing worked extraordinarily well in 1999—it was a time when people read all their emails.

Today, Instagram DMs still work for business development, but it's harder than it was in 2015 and 2016. You might have to be more strategic about who you're reaching out to, who you add into the message group, the number of people you reach out to, how established your own profile is, the opening line of your message, and other variables. Same thing with email marketing—it still works today, but you can't get 91 percent open rates on a 100,000-person email list like I did with WineLibrary.com in the late 1990s.

In 2019 and 2020, I was putting out a lot of content about why everyone should be making TikTok content. I was telling everyone that it's more than just kids lip-syncing and dancing—the platform offered enormous opportunities for brand awareness. The in-app content creation features were a relatively new thing back then, and I believed the app was like "training wheels" for future influencers and content creators. The content creation features made it easier for people to create, and I knew back then it would pave the way for other apps to integrate similar features. At that time, the opportunity for organic reach on TikTok was obnoxiously high, and it still is in 2023, but today it takes even better content to stand out (and it's not quite that obnoxious).

This has been a recurring theme over the last decade of social—first there's underpriced attention, and then, slowly but surely, people figure out the mismatch between supply and demand. First, it's usually entrepreneurs and creators who can move fast and experiment on new platforms without bureaucracy limiting their innovation. Sometime later, small businesses and startups begin to take advantage of the opportunity. Finally, big brands and advertising budgets eventually start flowing in. Then the supply and demand curve begins to even out—advertising ends up getting more expensive, and organic reach begins to stagnate or decline.

There's an especially big opportunity today for small businesses, entrepreneurs, and private-equity-owned brands. With so many Fortune 500 brands in the world continuing to allocate large budgets to outdated forms of advertising, there are still large gaps in supply of content across platforms. The faster you can understand and implement the strategies in this book, the more of an advantage you'll have in the current landscape of advertising. Although some advertising platforms are more mature than others, don't be confused: There's still a lot of organic reach and attention up for grabs. In my twenties, when I was buying wine terms on Google AdWords for ten cents a click, I initially thought that the opportunity was "over" once it was raised to a dollar. I thought competitors had "figured it out"—in hindsight, I made a huge mistake. Even a dollar was cheap.

Same thing with advertising platforms today. TikTok organic reach might not be as good as it was in 2020 (in fact, it's not even close), but there's still an enormous "land grab" of attention available. But just like you can't read about doing push-ups and get in great shape, you can't just read about marketing and magically grow your business.

If you want to take advantage of it, you must become a practitioner of day trading attention.

The insights and observations I'll share in this book are based on everything that my companies at VaynerX and I have learned over the years. At Vayner-Media, we've learned what successful marketing and advertising looks like for large Fortune 500 brands. Through the Sasha Group, we've helped small businesses grow and drive leads and revenue. Through VaynerCommerce, we've gained insights on scaling e-commerce and direct-to-consumer (DTC) companies. I continue to hold myself accountable to be a practitioner of everything I'm writing about—over the last decade, I've continued to grow the community around the GaryVee personal brand, as well as drive sales for Wine Library using modern marketing strategies. Many of these observations come from my personal interactions with thousands of startups, entrepreneurs, creators, and celebrities through my DMs on social. I've also gathered insights from other companies I've cofounded, such as Resy and Empathy Wines (Resy sold to American Express in 2019, and Empathy Wines sold to Constellation Brands in 2020). I've learned a lot from the companies I've invested in over the course of my career too, including Liquid Death, Slack, Coinbase, Venmo, Uber, Snap Inc., and more.

Day trading attention is what I do every day, and it's the reason I've had overall success in marketing over the course of my career of twenty-plus years. When I was a kid selling lemonade on Tingley Lane, day trading attention was about figuring out what trees to put signs on based on where drivers were most likely to look. When I was a teenager doing baseball card shows on the weekends, it was about setting up my display just right to catch the most eyes as people walked by. As a young adult working in my dad's liquor store, it was about studying customer movements throughout the store and learning the best wines to display near the cash register for deals. In my twenties and early thirties as we scaled the business, it was learning how to capture as many emails as possible, and knowing how to advertise on Google as more people began to search there.

Everything you'll see me talk about in this book comes from experience because I only talk about things I've lived. As new advertising mediums come out, the attention shifts, and the game continues, and this is a game I've been playing for many, many years.

The strategies in this book apply to companies of all sizes; you'll see different examples involving Fortune 1000 brands, influencers, local businesses, B2B companies, nonprofits, executives, direct-to-consumer companies, and more. As you get into the following pages, you'll also learn modern advertising tactics in deep detail. Platforms change rapidly, and it's possible that some of these tactics that work today as I'm writing this will not be as relevant by the time this book comes out. However, many other tactics here will be tried and true for the next several years and beyond, and the people who put them into practice will win.

I believe this book will create an enormous number of success stories, like *Crush It!* and *Jab, Jab, Jab, Right Hook*—I've written many books, and I know which ones I get the most emails about (gary@vaynerx.com). I look forward to hearing from you on how you put the strategies in this book into practice.

DAY TRADING
ATTENTION

PART 1

THE TIKTOKIFICATION
OF SOCIAL MEDIA

At thirty-two years old, I started getting involved in the world of social media and Web 2.0, as we called it then. I published Episode 1 of *Wine Library TV* in 2006 (a YouTube show where I tasted and reviewed wines—best gig I ever had), and shortly after, I started going to events like SXSW and getting acquainted with this emerging industry. Up until that point, I was a wine retailer, working every day to build my dad's business in an attempt to pay my family back for everything they did for me. At that time, I saw social media and tech as a totally new world of opportunity.

As I started going to more events and making connections, I became friends with several people on the 10–20 person Facebook team. I built relationships with other leaders in the Silicon Valley tech scene as well. I also started reading up on the budding world of Web 2.0 through resources like TechCrunch. I had a strong sense early on that social media would completely change the way human beings communicate, and I just wanted to be in the mix.

One day, I was presented with an opportunity to invest in a company called Twitter through a friendship I'd built over some time. (By the way, as I moved forward in finalizing that deal, I had to find a law firm in New Jersey to help with the process. I found one and came across a junior guy at the firm who was ascending to partner. He went by the name of Marc Yudkin, and he is now my COO at VaynerMedia, general counsel, and brother.)

Several months later, Randi Zuckerberg called me with an opportunity to buy some of her parents' Facebook stock. I said yes and wrote the biggest check I had ever written in my life, a six-figure check that pretty much wiped out all my savings at that time.

Finally, in that same year, David Karp and I became friends. I believed in his vision for his startup, Tumblr, and later ended up investing in it.

Facebook, Twitter, and Tumblr were the first three companies I ever invested in. Of course, this changed the trajectory of my life, but there's a funny reason why I tell this story:

When I invested in Tumblr, I called my brother and said, "AJ, Tumblr is going to be bigger than Facebook and Twitter. It's going to be the biggest one of them all."

AJ asked, "Why?"

I said, "On Facebook and Twitter, you follow people. On Tumblr, you follow things you're interested in."

Now, Tumblr didn't become the biggest of those three platforms, because there were so many other variables at play (although they still had a $1.1 billion exit to Yahoo in 2013). Still, that early realization about "interest"-based platforms versus "social"-based platforms is something that has continued to play out over time in a major way.

This speaks to why I was such a big advocate of Musical.ly early on. Released in 2014, Musical.ly was the first social platform that I saw since Tumblr that was distributing content to users based on their interests—something I will refer to as "the interest graph" for the rest of this book. I even had two Musical.ly stars come to my office for *AskGaryVee* Episode 198 in 2016 because I knew this platform was onto something. A year later in 2017, ByteDance acquired Musical.ly and merged it into TikTok in 2018. Since then, TikTok has been the largest champion of the interest graph model, and its execution of the "For You" page is something that I believe will define the foreseeable future of both social media and other advertising platforms—it already has.

Here's why it's so special:

At the time of writing, the default tab users land on when opening the app is the For You page. The content that TikTok surfaces there is based on the unique preferences of each user. TikTok considers videos you like or share, how long you watch videos, comments you post, and even the types of content you create. They also consider your device type, the location you're in, language preferences, and more—all these factors are processed by TikTok's recommendation engine and weighted based on how much you care about each specific factor. The algorithm learns each user's consumption patterns and adjusts their feed's content based on how those consumption patterns change over time.

In other words, their content feed is led by the interest graph (what you're interested in), rather than the social graph (who you follow).

Prior to TikTok's For You page, most platforms were led by the social graph. Some platforms still considered users' interests—Facebook, for example, used to have an algorithm called EdgeRank to determine what content would show up in user feeds. Every like, share comment, and new post from a user was counted as an "edge," and based on all those edges, Facebook would predict what types of content would be most interesting to that user. If you always "liked" a particular friend's photos but you skipped over their text-only status updates, the algorithm would show you more of that friend's photos and less of their status updates. Other platforms would consider user interests as well, but still, the content served would usually be within the container of who users decided to follow.

As social media matured, we soon found out that there were limitations to the "social graph"–driven content approach over time. When the content you see is based on which accounts you follow, it becomes harder to keep you on a platform as your relationships and preferences evolve over the course of your life. You might have subscribed to a YouTube channel in your early twenties about starting a company, but what happens at twenty-seven when those ambitions change? You might have followed some Facebook pages around your favorite artist in high school, but what happens when your music tastes shift? Within the social graph environment, you would have to actively follow new people or pages to get a steady stream of the content you want. It's higher friction and doesn't necessarily guarantee that you'd be seeing the content you want to see. An interest-graph-led algorithm, on the other hand, would automatically recognize your changing interests and show that content to you automatically, making it more likely that you'll stay on the platform longer.

At this point, nearly every platform is copying TikTok's interest-graph-led algorithm. Meta is making a huge interest graph push through Instagram Reels and Facebook Reels, as well as Instagram's Explore page. YouTube has expanded their video recommendation engine as well as their Shorts feed. X (Twitter) is making a push around their For You video feed, as well as their main For You feed that combines various post types. Snapchat is working on their Spotlight feature and LinkedIn is optimizing their own feed as well. It's a phenomenon I'm calling the "TikTokification of social media," and it has major implications for everyone reading this book.

For the first time ever, the incentives of businesses and the advertising channels are truly aligned. Think about it, Instagram doesn't want you to leave the app and go to YouTube Shorts. YouTube doesn't want to lose you to TikTok, and TikTok doesn't want to lose you to Netflix or Spotify. The war for attention is on, which means platforms are incentivized to distribute content that's relevant and valuable to the end consumer. This means that if you make content and advertising that people actually want to watch, you'll be rewarded with more views and engagement. The opportunity for organic reach is virtually unlimited. The more relevant your content is,

the more reach you'll get. This is a huge change, especially for the Madison Avenue advertising world. When a brand buys a billboard or a TV commercial spot, the advertising company doesn't just magically reward them with more impressions if their advertisement was good. Modern social platforms do. For example, if BMW makes a crappy ad to run on television, NBC won't care; they'll happily still take their money. The modern social platforms don't want users to make bad content, which makes them more aligned with the advertiser.

Prior to the TikTokification of social media, marketing on social platforms had a similar dynamic to email marketing. With email, you would spend time building a list, and then market to that list. Similarly, with social platforms, you would spend time building up your follower base and then you'd market to that follower base through your content. Much like email, only a small percentage of your social media audience would see each one of your posts. Now businesses, creators, and brands don't need to have a follower base before they can start getting views and engagement. You could create an account on any social platform in this book today, post some content over the course of this week, and you actually have a shot at getting thousands, tens of thousands, hundreds of thousands, or even millions of views. It just depends on whether your content is good enough or not. Learn to make compelling, relevant content at scale and the platform will distribute your content to people who are interested in consuming it.

Even with my millions of followers on TikTok, if I post a piece of content no one wants to watch, it might only get a few thousand views. Meanwhile, if a car dealership with fifteen followers posts a video relevant to people who want to buy cars, it might get millions of views and have people coming to the dealership from different parts of the state. Similarly, if a regular guy working at a potato factory posts a lighthearted video drinking Ocean Spray juice on his longboard, it just might change his entire life—that is the power of the TikTokification of social media.

You potentially could get 100 views, then 10,000 on your next piece of content, then back to 300 on the next ten, then up to 500,000 on the following one, etc. That's what happens when the creative is the variable of success, not the number of followers you have (by the way,

the words *creative* and *content* mean the same thing; I'll use them interchangeably in this book). Of course, these numbers may vary based on the platform. Certain platforms may still place higher value on how many followers you have than others—not every platform's interest graph algorithm is as advanced as TikTok's at the time of this writing, but I believe variability in views on each piece of content you post will only get wider and wider over time. Every platform is moving in this direction.

This puts small businesses and creators on a much more even playing field with larger companies, which means major brands now have to worry about small companies taking their market share. Beverage brands across the board have to compete with Logan Paul and KSI's Prime Hydration. Folgers has to compete with Chamberlain Coffee. In this new social media world, a creator who truly understands how to capture attention could start a skin-care line tomorrow that competes with the biggest names in the industry.

Today, people who know how to make great content will have a leg up on big brands, many of which are still trying to pass off overproduced television ads as social media content. In fact, I predict that over the next ten to fifteen years, human-based consumer brands will become the biggest issue for the largest consumer brands in the world (that was the journey I went on with Empathy Wines back in 2019 and the journey that

Mr. Beast is currently on with Feastables at a bigger scale).

Everyone is competing for the same, limited space in the user's feed, and the best way to win that space is by making more relevant content. More relevance equals more reach.

Advertising in the World of the Interest Graph

So, if relevance is what we all need to be aiming at, how do we know what kinds of content would be the most relevant to the end user? How do we know what kinds of content people actually want to consume, and what will get the most meaningful distribution?

Fortunately, you don't have to guess. With interest-graph-driven algorithms, you can find out the truth for yourself for zero additional cost (beyond what it takes to make the creative itself). Make a piece of content based on who you want to reach and what you think they might be interested in seeing, post it on one or more platforms of your choice, and look at your post analytics and comments to see what happens. Did it do better than your account's average performance? Did it do worse? Who did the platform

end up serving it to, based on your analytics (in other words, who was *actually* interested in consuming it versus who you *thought* would be interested in consuming it)? Any interesting observations in the comments? You can use all these observations to make your next piece of content even better.

This is a game changer, especially for large brands. Currently, they might spend months defining guidelines for the content and ads they want to put out, between defining their target audience, doing research, conducting focus groups, selling ideas through various internal decision makers, and more. The process is slow, outdated, and built for those developing TV commercials in the pre–social media era. Brands would decide to spend $8 million on a commercial (between agency fees, production costs, and media costs), and use a combination of their research and subjective opinions to make a generic thirty-second video that would appeal to the various demographics that watch it.

Today, with interest graph algorithms, instead of putting months and months of research, effort, and resources into a TV commercial that people will most likely not watch, brands can put out content (aka ads) every day based on a hypothesis of what will work and get actual results to validate or invalidate their hypothesis. They can rely on reactions from the market, instead of ten people in a focus group.

For example, let's say you're leading marketing efforts for a large athletic clothing brand, and you want to make a TV commercial to get more moms across the US to buy your clothing. You can make 20, 30, 40+ different pieces of content/ads for narrow demographics of moms, post them across social media platforms, and see what happens. Observe what pieces of content perform better than the average on your account, see who ends up consuming the piece of content through post analytics, note what words and messaging catch atten-

tion, and use those learnings to help craft your higher-production, higher-budget commercials.

It's similar to how stand-up comedians try out different material. They go in front of smaller crowds at a bunch of different comedy clubs, see what lines work and with whom they work, and use those learnings to make their next show even better. By the time they do a big Netflix comedy special, there's very little guessing involved; they already know what to do. Similarly, learnings from social media marketing can help brands mitigate risk on higher-production campaigns.

I call this "marketing for the sake of better marketing." You do actual marketing with the goal of building brand and sales through social media, and you also use those learnings from content to do even better marketing in the future. The confusion is that companies approach these social media posts (again, which are advertisements) with a mindset of "test and learn," "throw it against the wall and see what sticks," or "spray and pray." Just to remind you: This is marketing for the sake of better marketing.

This applies to creators and small businesses too. Say you have a business with $250 a month to spend on paid advertising. Instead of debating what content to run as an ad this month, you can post a bunch of organic content, see which ones resonate, and turn those pieces of content into ads to drive sales (aka "brandformance"). If the content already did well when you posted it organically, you have more proof that it'll work when you run it as an ad, mitigating your risk.

As you'll see in this book, the amount of data available across social platforms is immense. For example, at the time of writing, you can see how many people viewed your video versus swiped away on YouTube Shorts. You can see average watch time on your TikTok videos. You can see how many followers versus nonfollowers viewed your Instagram and Facebook Reels. You can even see the job titles of individuals who consumed your content on LinkedIn. You can track metrics like views, saves, shares, likes, and comments on certain platforms to see how people engaged with your content.

There are many ways to use this data.

For example, large brands can make skits on TikTok featuring different potential mascots with a variety of character traits. They can observe reactions in the comments before building the mascot into a much bigger part of the brand. Think GEICO using content to test Martin the Gecko against the GEICO Caveman to see which character resonated with people the best. E-commerce companies can make TikToks with sample items they're thinking of selling and decide whether to carry inventory after seeing whether people are interested in the product. If a local restaurant is debating what new menu item to add, they could make a video asking that question, run it as a Facebook ad to their local area, and use community feedback as a data point in making the decision.

In the new social media world, everything is about the content itself, not the people who chose to follow you. Creative is the variable of success.

PART 2

THE MODERN ADVERTISING FRAMEWORK

There are two ways to invest: You can either make long-term bets, go to sleep, and wait for the returns to show up over time, or you can day trade. Both are different ways to do it. Marketing *used* to be like the former—brands would spend months planning out a campaign, execute on traditional channels like television, and bet on the fact that it'll work out. Today marketing is like day trading—if you are not staying ahead of the curve every day, somebody is outflanking you. That means your strategies need to be far more sophisticated than ever.

In part 3, I'll go into extreme detail on the six core variables to win in this new environment. Your level of success will largely depend on how deeply you understand these variables, and how you incorporate them into your advertising strategy. It's why part 3 is the deepest section in this book; I'm giving you all the details.

Before we get there, though, here's an overview of the core variables that make up the modern advertising framework—later you'll see how they all work together:

Cohort development: Defining who you want to reach

When you're making content, the first step is to develop cohorts. This term refers to the buckets of often narrow but sometimes broad consumer segmentations that you'd want to try to reach.

Platforms and Culture (PAC): The new requirement for your advertising knowledge

PAC is a two-pronged framework that should inform the content you create. First, you have to know the platforms, or more specifically, the creative units and features on the platforms you're posting on. By creative units, I mean the *types* of creative you can post on each platform; on Instagram, some of the creative units are stories, Reels, and carousels. You have to know the nuances of these creative units. For example, how long can an Instagram Reel be? Do you know which creative units are getting the most organic reach on each platform? Do you know how carousels on LinkedIn, Instagram, and TikTok appear differently infeed? The reason this is important is that it helps you ideate your content; if you know that a LinkedIn carousel has to be uploaded as a PDF document, whereas an Instagram carousel is uploaded as a series of images or videos directly in the app, then that will impact your ideation around each piece of creative.

The other aspect of PAC is culture. Are there any current events related to your business category that your cohorts would know about? What influencers and celebrities might your cohorts be following? Do you know how to speak to your cohorts, based on their interests and slang?

Strategic organic content (SOC): What good modern advertising looks like

SOC is the content that you post across platforms to build relevance, brand, and sales. I added the *S* in SOC because content must be strategic. SOC is about the small details, such as what the first three seconds look like, what your copy (aka the post caption) says, the title text you add on the video, how long your video is, and more. PAC knowledge can help you make more strategic organic content.

Amplification: Spending against what works, aka not wasting a penny

Amplification refers to any tactic that lets you reach even more people through your content. That means running paid ads on social platforms, running ads on streaming services, influencer marketing, TV commercials, outdoor media, and more. The content you decide to amplify would be informed by SOC insights: What pieces are overperforming? Which ones are getting more comments? For example, you could decide to take a piece of overperforming strategic organic content, add some sales-focused elements, and run it as a brandformance ad with some slight tweaks, since you know the content has already been validated by the interest graph algorithm.

Videos people want to watch: Modern commercials

These are more broadly relatable, higher-production videos that you can make (depending on your resources). Unlike traditional commercials, modern-day commercials are pieces of content that don't feel like an "ad." People actually want to watch them, and the production is always informed by insights and observations from the content (aka SOC) you're putting out across platforms. Please note: This is a video that looks like a skit from a sitcom, a music video, a

movie trailer, a *Saturday Night Live* skit. The videos that people actually want to watch in the world.

Post-creative strategy (PCS): Listening to actual consumers and gathering insights

Post-creative strategy is all about listening. Once strategic organic content gets posted, read the comments on your content and comments on other accounts that are relevant to who you're trying to reach. This way, you'll get a better sense for what's resonating, what isn't, and who your content is reaching. PCS insights help make your next piece of SOC even better, and help you uncover new cohorts or eliminate existing cohorts as needed.

In a nutshell, that's the framework. Define who you want to reach, use platform knowledge and cultural insights to make strategic content, and leverage insights from data and comments to decide what ads to run, and what to build on further with higher-production pieces of content.

The following graphic illustrates the overall process:

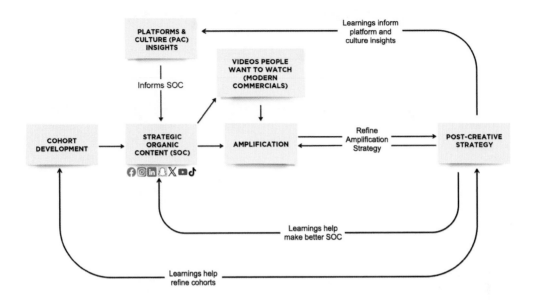

To give you a little preview of what this process looks like in action, here's a simple example:

Let's say you have a small business that sells kids' clothing. How would you use the modern advertising framework to build brand and drive sales?

Before you jump into running ads, throwing money into a high-production commercial, or even making content, you need to get a sense for 1) who you want to reach, and 2) what those people care about so you can make the kind of advertising they actually *want* to consume. By now, you know that if people are interested in consuming your advertising,

you'll stay relevant and top of mind. Relevance is what leads to consideration, and eventually sales.

The first step is identifying a variety of different consumer segments (or cohorts), so that you can make advertising that's relevant to them (rather than something generic that's meant to appeal to everyone). Based on your business objectives, maybe you decide to focus on millennial moms who recently had their first kid and dads who have young daughters (aka girl dads), among thirty to forty other cohorts.

Next, go into each platform and do some research on what these cohorts

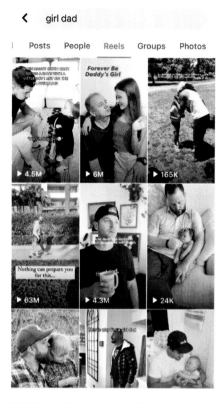

(Left) "Girl dad" search on TikTok. (Right) "Girl dad" search on Facebook Reels. August 12, 2023.

naturally watch and engage with. With platforms' search capabilities constantly improving, you can type in something like "girl dad" in the search bar and find videos relevant to that group.

Spend some time going through hashtags and search results. Notice what creative formats and styles are overperforming. Notice what's underperform-

ing. Notice how the content differs across platforms. Are people using similar wording in the titles of their videos? Are they using the same audio? Are people using certain platform features such as duets, polls, or video replies to comments? What kinds of content are companies and brands posting? What kinds of content are actual human beings posting?

These platform and culture (PAC) insights will inform what your strategic organic content (SOC) might look like. Instead of blindly making content in a spray-and-pray manner, you can first narrow in on:

1. Your creative unit (such as a standard TikTok video, as opposed to a carousel or photo)
2. Your creative format (such as filming a TikTok video with "pov: you're a girl dad" in the title), and
3. Platform features you want to use (such as TikTok's content creation tools to type out the title in-app, as opposed to adding it through a different video editing software).

If you click on some of the videos titled "pov: you're a girl dad" from the search results on the previous page you might notice many of them have a similar style. At the time of writing, many of them feature dads with their wives and daughters, and the camera angle alternates between them as they lip-sync parts of a song. You could decide to make a similar video; or if you're not a dad with daughters and there's no one in your company who can help, you could start with a different creative format. For example, on the next page you'll find a video from an apparel shop with the title "pov: taking a shower when you're a girl dad," which is a short video of a guy walking into a shower and stepping over a bunch of bath care products.

Maybe you could try a few variations based on common situations that girl dads experience; some variations could tie in your kids' clothing product in a creative way, and others could be more broadly relatable for girl dads.

Once you know *what* you want to make, you can then execute with strategic organic content principles in mind. For example, if you know you're making a TikTok video, with SOC knowledge you'd know you need to capture attention right away in the first three seconds. This might mean your title needs to be relatable and placed at the beginning, so people know right away what the video is about. You might also add certain camera angles, cuts, and movements in the early part of the video to keep people watching. If you're making the same video for Snapchat, SOC would look different; maybe you change the title to make it more relatable for young people as opposed to dads and add it in-app in Snapchat's native style. Please note: Snapchat

has not aged up in its content platform in the way TikTok has. I know many of you reading this probably have Snapchat and TikTok in the same place demographic-wise, but they're considerably different. The consumption on TikTok has aged up far more in the directions we've seen historically from Facebook and Instagram, while Snapchat, because it's used more as a messaging platform for the youth, has stayed quite young. Thus, the people we're targeting in the content part of Snapchat Spotlight and Discover skew younger.

If a piece of content you post resonates (which you can measure based on how many views it gets compared to the average on your account, the type of engagement it gets, how many sales you get as a result of posting it organically, or other indicators), the next step is to amplify it. If the girl dad video hit, that means you now have a piece of content that has proven to work. You could amplify it through an ad on TikTok, for example. You could repurpose the piece of content into a Facebook ad, potentially layer on some ad targeting (such as men in the US who are parents of preschoolers ages three to five), and see if it resonates there too. You could use tools like TikTok Creator Marketplace or YouTube BrandConnect to partner with influencers in the "parenting" category, who could take the learnings from your organic content success and build on it with similar content advertising your products.

Depending on your resources, you could also create more broadly relatable, "modern commercials" using the learnings from your strategic organic content. Maybe you posted twenty-five different videos with relatable scenarios for girl dads similar to the examples above, such as "pov: you're a girl dad getting ready in the morning," "pov: you're a girl dad coming back from work," "pov: you're a girl dad watching the game," and more. If you noticed three or four of those get more traction than the rest, you could build those out into a funny skit made for increased distribution that's geared toward a broader audience of parents, for example, with direct-response elements like a QR code at the end to drive traffic to your site. You could also make a different version of the same video sending people to the URL that's in your ac-

count (such as, driving to a "link in bio" on Instagram) instead of a QR code, as an alternative, lower-friction approach to drive traffic to your URL.

Contextual versions of that video could go on YouTube as well as other platforms, depending on the length of the skit along with other SOC and PAC elements. You could amplify it further through YouTube pre-roll ads targeted at "in-market audiences" related to kids' clothing (Google's way of identifying people who are in-market to purchase). You could run it as a commercial on over-the-top (OTT) streaming services like Hulu, connected TV devices like Roku, or free ad-supported streaming television (FAST) channels like Pluto TV. Although detailed targeting capabilities on these platforms are still being developed, and your cost per thousand impressions (CPMs) might be higher than on social media, you can spend with a little more confidence knowing that your content has been validated already. One of the key characteristics of this form of advertising is to use social media for both quantitative and qualitative insights on actual consumer beliefs around your creative, therefore mitigating the risk when you take it to bigger and more expensive formats and distributions.

Throughout the entire process, you'll be reading the comments on every one of your posts and paying close attention to consumer behavior across your cohort segmentations. This level of listening is what I call post-creative strategy. These are the insights that help make your next piece of content even better than your last. For example, reading the comments could help you pick up on inside jokes that only girl dads would get, which could then lead to a new piece of SOC. It could help you uncover new cohorts you may not have considered; maybe you notice *daughters* of girl dads leaving comments about how much they relate to those videos. Maybe you realize they're the ones driving some of the above-average distribution of your videos by sending it to their dads. You can add them to your cohort list, do research on the content they like to consume, post a few pieces of SOC for them made for shareability, and go through the rest of the process as needed. You might even notice some comments that spark ideas for new products, collaborations with other brands, partnerships with certain influencers, or lead to new terminology/slang that you use in your copywriting in future posts.

Makes sense?

The same framework works for large brands too. Let's take a different example—say you're leading marketing for a national brand in the consumer packaged goods (CPG) space, and you want to drive in-store sales. You want more customers to walk into places like Kroger and Walmart and buy your product off the shelf. How would you use this framework to do that?

You could start by looking at your business objectives to determine your cohort categories.

Based on the store locations your brand is in, you could narrow in on areas that have strong potential for sales growth (such as areas where your brand isn't as developed but your category is established with high demand, and areas where you have strong distribution). Depending on your business, there may be other factors you consider as well, but the main thing is to find the areas where you're most likely to get the highest sales increase for your marketing investment.

Then you can break down who you're trying to reach at a more granular level. If you're selling environmentally friendly cleaning products, maybe you make content for 25–29-year-old women in Los Angeles interested in sustainability;

maybe you make content for 45–50-year-old moms in Chattanooga who wear sustainable clothing. You could do the same across all your key store locations. Cohorts could be informed by your existing sales data in each region, such as who's buying your products, how much potential you have in each market to get more of those customers, or if you need to win over a different demographic segment.

Once you have 20, 30, 40+ consumer segmentations, you can then go into each advertising platform and start getting a feel for the creative units and content formats that these groups want to consume. You can gather PAC insights to help inform what "consumer centric" content actually looks like. Just like how we searched "girl dad" on TikTok and Facebook Reels in the prior example, you could search things like "sustainable fashion" or "Chattanooga parents" and see what pops up. You can see what cultural references different groups are using, what songs they're listening to, and gather other information you can then use to make strategic organic content.

A lot of Fortune 500 brands struggle with this because of their own internal, subjective interpretations of what "qual-ity" content looks like. Many of them overly stick to their "brand guidelines" and make content that subjectively fits the brand's persona, instead of what people want to consume. Companies are convinced that it's not "on brand" to post content with different fonts, colors, thumbnails, and product use cases, but the reality is, these restrictions just make their content less interesting. Brands should think about how they can convey different messages to different people instead of trying to force the same formats and messaging in all their ads. People will only consider buying something if it means something to them. The only way to make a brand meaningful is to make it relevant to as many different people as possible. I call this being "boardroom centric" versus being "consumer centric." It's the biggest issue facing the biggest brands in the world today. Until the past is debated more properly through a contemporary consumer behavior lens, the biggest brands in the world will continue to lose market share to many of the brands that are going to be started by the people who read this book.

Once you're making SOC for your consumer segments, next is constantly paying attention to your analytics and your comments to see which ones are hitting. If you're targeting 45–50-year-old moms in Los Angeles interested in sustainable clothing, you could make a video for them, add a Los Angeles location tag, make city-specific references in your video, and your content may actually get organically distributed to users in the city.

Next comes amplification. If the North Star for your CPG brand is to get more households to buy your product, one option (out of many) is to turn your overperforming organic content into ads on Facebook and Instagram with the goal of maximizing reach. You could target 45–50-year-old moms interested in sustainable clothing within a five-mile radius of the store that carries your product. If your goal is more reach, the platform will show your ads to as many people as possible within your designated target (at the time of writing). If your content already resonated with that group organically, there's potentially less risk of missing the mark when you amplify the content with a goal like reach. In your ad content, you could incentivize people to go to the store, and even take

photos and share them on their own socials with a hashtag so you can use that for additional content.

Media dollars especially matter in situations like this when you're trying to get sales with customers in a specific local area because your organic content may not reach people within the city alone, so targeting your overperforming content within your select local regions becomes especially important.

This new way of running media is based on actual consumer intent—instead of relying on the subjective opinions of internal decision makers to make important media buying decisions, you can use consumer data from both organic and paid social media to drive some of your more expensive, higher-produced ad campaigns.

In this specific scenario, you could also potentially go on Instagram, type in each of your store locations in the search bar, scroll through top posts in the area, and find local influencers whom you can pay to do meet-and-greets at your stores (assuming the retailer would allow you to do that, which many don't).

Based on the content that's resonating in organic, paid social, and influencer campaigns, you can turn those into higher-production, modern commercials on OTT and CTV (connected TV) devices targeting your store location zip codes, outdoor media near your stores, or traditional television if you're buying remnant inventory and cost makes sense.

With Roku and Instacart's recent partnership before this writing, CPG brands can run ads on Roku and see whether people bought on Instacart after seeing the ad. With platforms like the Trade Desk, brands can buy premium inventory on major networks and streaming services, and even use first-party data (information collected from your customer base or subscribers) for more precise targeting. With these modern-day ad platforms, you can use consumer insights to make commercials with direct-response focus that people actually want to watch. You can build brand and sales at the same time.

When it comes to attribution, you can look at actual sales reports from your stores to see whether your strategy worked. You can look at incremental sales numbers of the stores in locations you made content for and compare them against other stores that you didn't drive foot traffic to. If you keep other variables constant (that is, you don't drive sales through discounts and you don't change your product's placement in the stores), then you'll know whether building brand and relevance is leading to sales instead of relying on brand lift studies or other "proxy reports."

Let's take another example. This time, say you're running a local arts nonprofit, and every summer you put on a series of shows in your small town featuring artwork done by kids in the area. Your goal is to drive more donations, and you don't have money or resources. How would you get more donors?

When you don't have a lot of time or content creation resources, the biggest thing to do is set up a system where you record long-form content that can then be chopped up into clips that you can post across platforms. For a lot of people, starting a weekly podcast is the most practical way to do that. In this situation, the number one thing is to film the art shows from as many angles as possible because that will be the footage that you use for your advertising content. If the show is open for a few hours and people are just walking through, you'd want to walk out of there knowing that you have 40, 50, 70+ moments that you can use for content. Remember, you don't need a high-budget super camera from Hollywood—there are plenty of cameras that can get the job done, including the one on your phone.

During the show, it's important for the founder or someone else from the organization to go around and interview people, asking questions that have potential to overperform as social media content. This is where understanding cohort segments becomes valuable. If you know that your most common donors are 40–50-year-old parents living in your town, then maybe you can interview those kinds of people as they're walking through the show or ask questions that are interesting to that demographic. When you postproduce that content and post those clips across platforms, other 40–50-year-old parents in your area may feel more affinity toward your organization when they see people who look like them right away in the first three seconds of the video (potentially people they even know).

There are two main reasons for interviewing people at the show: 1) It saves you time, so you can rely on the show footage for content rather than coming up with new ideas on your own, and 2) if you scroll through your feeds across social, chances are you'll see some clips where two people are doing Q&A with one another out in public. These "street interviews" can be appealing because they come off as authentic and real, and this creative format may get more distribution as a result.

As you're asking questions, think of what you can ask that the broader public may be interested in. Instead of just asking "Did you have a good time here?" or "What was your favorite part of the show?" (which can still be useful to gather testimonials and reviews), also ask questions about what their favorite memory was from their own art class growing up. Ask about a funny story that happened, or their "art nightmare" from school. Ask fun questions like "What color paint are you and why?" Ask questions that could lead to greater distribution, ones that get more organic reach than your standard pieces of content.

This kind of relatable content could do well across Facebook, Instagram, TikTok, Snapchat, X (Twitter), YouTube Shorts, LinkedIn, and YouTube long form. When you post-edit the footage for each platform, that's where SOC and PAC knowledge come into play. Maybe you connect with a bunch of parents from your town on LinkedIn and post videos from your personal profile; if you believe that they're likely donors, then connecting with them on LinkedIn would make it more likely that they'll see your posts.

As you're editing with SOC in mind, you could try a few different variations of your videos: Some clips could start off with a fun question in the first three seconds, like "What was the craziest story from art class growing up?" If the person being interviewed gave a wild response, you could do another version of the video where you start with their answer instead of your question, post both versions across platforms (tweaking the copy for each platform so it's contextual), and gather insights on what worked and what didn't. If one version did overperform your averages on Facebook Reels but underperformed on YouTube, then you could dig into the analytics and comments and start thinking about why.

For nonprofits specifically, it's worth considering how direct you want to be with asking for donations in your organic content. Maybe 50 percent of your content could be about building general awareness around what your organization does (which would lead to people clicking into your profile and visiting your donation page on their own), and 50 percent of your content could literally ask for donations directly in the copy or in the last few frames of your video. Every nonprofit should play with their own ratios here, but no one should be 100 percent in either direction.

In this scenario, if you've been getting 50 to 100 views on your Instagram account on average over the previous months of posting organically, but three of your new clips from the show got 400 to 500 views each, then you can consider amplifying those with paid advertising. You could spend $100 on three clips and run them as Instagram video ads with a goal of driving donations (with your copy asking people to donate in a very direct way). You could target them against everyone in the ten-mile radius of your town and rely on the algorithm to find the people most likely to convert.

Does this all feel like a lot to consider so far?

Between developing cohorts, making strategic organic content, applying insights about platforms and culture, creating modern-day commercials, learning amplification strategies, and doing post-creative strategy, I have empathy for how it can seem like a lot. The problem is that this is the reality of what it takes to be successful in the modern advertising environment.

So, where should you start? If you're in a full-time job right now and you want to build a business around your passion for cooking, what's step one?

First, I think everybody gets too caught up in trying to boil the ocean. As you continue reading this book, understand that you shouldn't have all of this figured out at once. Long before you can dunk a basketball, you must learn how to walk and not shit your pants.

As you go through this book start to finish, think about what comes most naturally to you and which skills you're most interested in developing. If you're good at staying tapped into cultural trends, then start there. Even if your videos aren't strategically produced with platform nuances in mind, they'll still do decent if you're making smart cultural references. If you're a little more type A and you love learning about strategy (such as what the first three seconds of your video should look like, or optimizing your video based on watch-time analytics and retention graphs), then start there.

If you want to quit your full-time job to pursue your passion for cooking, the first thing I would do is just start making food content. Take as much as you can from this book and implement it. After posting consistently (multiple times a day for several weeks or months), then you can start challenging yourself to incorporate more elements and variables that you hadn't before.

Think of it like working out. When you first start working out, maybe you just want to get your stamina up on the treadmill. Then you start working on your muscles with the lowest weight that you can lift. As you keep going, you can start doing more challenging workouts with more weight. But in the early days, you just have to get yourself to the gym.

It's no different when it comes to being a prolific content creator and advertiser. Just start.

PART 3

THE CORE VARIABLES

Cohort Development: Defining Who You Want to Reach

Before you make a piece of content or any ad, the most important question to ask yourself is "Why am I making this?" That's why cohort development is the step that we start with.

Cohorts are labels that describe any current customers or clients, potential customers or clients, and give you a framework for what content to create. This way, instead of serving a

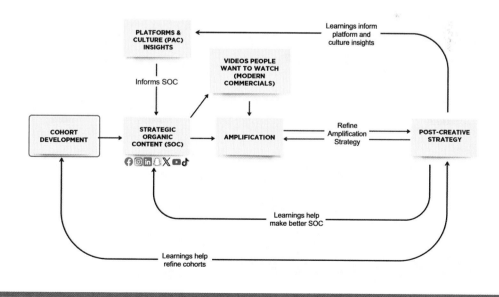

DAY TRADING ATTENTION

single message to a mass audience, you can make content that's relevant to each individual cohort. If you were serving ice cream to a large crowd, you wouldn't just give everybody vanilla, because people like different flavors. Cohort development is about defining different audience segments, so you know what "flavors" to serve them.

When brands make commercials for traditional television, it's hard to make them with specific cohorts in mind because the network's audience is usually very broad. On social platforms, however, we can make content for a variety of different cohorts because contemporary interest-graph-driven algorithms will serve it to whoever wants to watch it. We can create brand relevance through that content, and potentially also use insights from it to inform traditional TV commercials, outdoor media campaigns, or other contemporary marketing efforts—instead of the other way around (that is, making generic TV commercials for a broad viewership, and using those same assets for social media).

A few things to consider when defining your cohorts are:

I. Define cohorts with "teeth."

For example, instead of 18–35-year-old males, what if you made content for 18–22-year-old males living in New York who are into basketball? Instead of 20–35-year-old professionals, what if you made content for 25–30-year-old females in LA making over $75,000 a year? Instead of 30–45-year-old moms, what if you made content for 40–45-year-old moms in Singapore who have an affinity to high fashion? I call these "cohorts with teeth"—in other words, specific segmentations that give you the opportunity to create more relevant content. A twenty-one-year-old guy in New York who's into basketball will respond to a very different piece of creative than a twenty-year-old guy in Tennessee who goes hiking every weekend. Grouping them both into the bucket of 18–35-year-old males doesn't give as big an opportunity to make them care about your brand or business.

This especially applies to large brands that are at national scale that need every human being to know about them. Take an iconic brand like Nike, for example. Advertisers may think everyone associates Nike with "Just Do It," but that's not true. Some people buy their sneakers because of the brand's association with street culture. Some people buy it because they're fans of Virgil Abloh. Others buy from the brand because they like to go to the outlet store thirty minutes away from their city in a rural suburb and get a good deal on sweatpants. Brands can have different meanings for different people; defining cohorts with teeth can help you achieve that.

2. Think of your cohorts like an "accordion."

If you have a retail store that sells primarily to a female customer base, you might initially think that your cohort segments would all be women. But after putting out ten to twenty pieces of content, maybe you notice in the comments that husbands of female shoppers are secretly excited about being dragged along to your store. With that observation, you could make content for them with the hypothesis that maybe they'll share it with their wives and they'll both feel fonder toward your store as a result. You could then define a new cohort with "teeth" that represents husbands of your female shoppers.

Another example: Maybe you put out a few pieces of content aimed at 18–22-year-old males into basketball in New York, but you notice in the comments that you're getting meaningful engagement from people referencing the Knicks. You might decide to tweak that cohort to 18–22-year-old male Knicks fans in New York. Or you might look at the analytics for the post and notice that it's being served in a whole different city altogether, which means you can then hypothesize why the piece of content resonated more broadly. Based on actual results and engagement from your pieces of content, you can add, remove, or adjust your segmentations as needed.

Since your cohorts will always be shrinking, expanding, and changing based on your post-creative strategy insights from the comments (which I'll explore in more detail later), I like to think of them as an accordion. In fact, it's quite common for us at VaynerMedia to eliminate some cohorts we're working with altogether after one to four months or so and stand up two to four other new cohorts that came from insights from the comments section.

3. Consider the business objectives of your company.

Look at consumer segments that you've historically done well with, or areas where you intuitively know you need to grow. If "moms 27–35 in Salt Lake City" have bought from you repeatedly, then maybe you want to double down on that and go even narrower within that segment: such as moms 27–35 in Salt Lake City who are into yoga, or high-income moms who have a house in Park City, Utah.

If you believe your product should be doing better with certain consumer segmentations, you can lean into those too.

Let's say you're a content creator who does card tricks, and you have ambitions to sell out a show in Las Vegas one day. Say your current audience consists of young males. In this case, you'd need to create cohorts like 40–46-year-old moms in Chicago. Why? Because that will dictate the ideation of your content and will help you make different stuff that will resonate with different people. If you know you're making content for 40–46-year-old moms in Chicago with teenage sons, the content you're going to make will attempt to appeal to that mom

as opposed to the algorithm, what you think is the viral trend of the moment, or what your friends and other young men are going to like. It completely changes the starting point for the ideation of your creative, therefore allowing your brand to broaden. Now you'd be trying to find a mom in a mall to do a magic trick for, and after the act, you could ask a quick question like "Just an extra minute for my TikTok, what's the toughest thing about raising a son?" That piece of content might help new audiences find you and become interested in you.

4. Define a high volume of cohorts.

Many brands only define a handful of broad cohorts, which often results in generic creative that isn't meaningful to the audience that's consuming. The more cohorts you define, the more opportunities you have to create relevance for your business or brand. Based on results from your content, you can always add or remove cohorts.

One important note, especially for high-end brands in the luxury category, is that making content for more people doesn't mean you have to compromise on your production value. Just because your photo shoot or video shoot was done on a cattle ranch because you're trying to win with that demographic doesn't mean that you're compromising the quality of the content or the quality of your product. For luxury brands specifically, I would argue that they could benefit from a little bit more casual content scattered throughout to make them more approachable and humbler. That being said, I'm incredibly empathetic after being in boardrooms with many of the biggest luxury brands in the world that that's not going to happen anytime soon. That's unfortunate because what luxury brands have done over the last twenty years with streetwear brand collaborations has broadened their appeal dramatically; their narrow focus on the subjective opinions on the production value of their content on social media is limiting their opportunity to grow their business. Very few people will be turned off by their "human" content, and many more will finally consider buying from them because the content will feel more relevant and approachable to them.

When you make content for a variety of different cohorts, you're trading on the context, not the production value. This is something a lot of high-end brands struggle with; as a whole, they don't do as much content with a wide range of consumer segments because they think it compromises the brand. In reality, I think it has a lot more to do with the internal politics at the organizations, and the desire of creative directors to stay in control—not that it's an impossible task from the brand's standpoint.

It's true that sometimes you need to say "no" to making certain types of content to preserve a brand. I value "no" very much, but when you only say "yes" four out of four thousand times, your balance is off. Everything's best in balance. The social media creative conversation with luxury brands is very clear to me: They are truly treating it like fashion shows and *Vogue* print ads, and they're missing a lot of opportunities.

5. The creative you produce could hit multiple cohorts.

The methodology here isn't always linear. Sometimes you might think of a piece of content you want to try out that doesn't clearly fall into one cohort or might fall into multiple. You might have a piece of content that you just really want to make, or an idea that multiple different cohorts might be interested in. Cohort labels are just hypotheses that you can come back to and refine later—don't be crippled by content that could fall into multiple buckets.

6. Consider (but don't overthink) media addressability.

Media addressability (the total number of people you can reach in your ad targeting through paid advertising) is another factor to consider when defining who you want to make creative for. As you make content that overperforms organically, you might want to amplify some down the road and run them as paid social media ads; in that case, how would you target them?

As platform algorithms continue to evolve, they continue to get better at automatically serving your ads to the best possible cohorts based on who they think will engage with it. You might think that you're trying to reach 18–22-year-old males in Missouri who are interested in gaming, but platforms might pick up on the fact that you're getting higher watch time and conversion from a different segment that you

may not have expected and serve your ads to them instead. This can happen both in organic content as well as paid advertising. Remember—even though you're creating all these narrow cohorts, when you're posting organically, you wouldn't be manually targeting them through the platform anyway. You'd be relying on the algorithm to help you find the right audience.

Also, to remind you, a big reason to define cohorts with teeth in the first place is to give you a strong framework for creative ideation to make unique content. It's not that you're *only* going to reach that audience and no one else. By defining narrow cohorts, your content is going to be more unique, sharper, more specific, and more relatable to different people. Too many people today make too much generic content. Too much of the same stuff. By going narrow, you win.

Let's say you have a local accounting firm, and you noticed a lot of sign-ups on your website after you posted a video titled "5 things business owners don't know about taxes" on your Facebook page. When you amplify the video as a paid ad, instead of targeting "business owners" in your town, you could target everyone in your town and surrounding towns, while trusting that the algorithm will optimize distribution and show your ad to the right people who will sign up on your website. The creative would remain the same—your content would still technically be geared toward business owners even though your targeting is broader. That way, you give yourself room for serendipity—you might find that people who have full-time jobs with side hustles are also watching your ad and signing up. Facebook might identify any number of variations of cohorts that want to consume your ad—cohorts that you might not have expected.

However, there's no universal right answer on whether your media targeting should be narrow or broad. Depending on the platform, you could try both; for example, if you have a B2B SaaS (software as a service) company, you might define one of your cohorts as chief information officers at the specific companies you're trying to reach. You can make content specifically for those organizations, and use LinkedIn to run ads to executives at those companies with very specific, narrow targeting. There might also

be scenarios when you want to target people within your own audience, such as people from your customer database or everyone who watched a certain percentage of an Instagram video.

As we'll explore later in the "Amplification" section, different platforms have different levels of sophistication in their algorithm, which also plays a role here.

7. Consider subcultures, stages of life people are at, affinities and passions, psychographics, cultural trends, and more.

There are many ways to define cohorts—age, geographic location, and interests are just a few of the many factors to consider. What about millennial parents working from home and feeling burntout? What about graduating college students feeling anxious about entering the "real world"? What about 40–50-year-olds who reached a breaking point with their health and are committed to working out more? What about the emerging trends around young people not drinking alcohol and preferring mocktails instead? This is where knowledge of cultural trends is required.

Platforms and Culture (PAC): The New Requirement for Your Advertising Knowledge

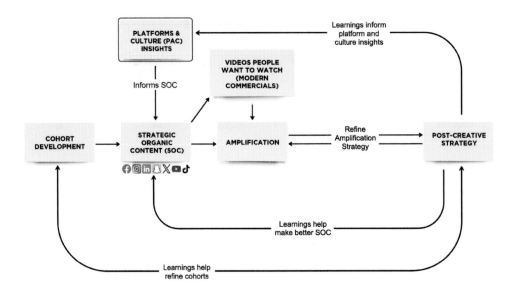

PAC refers to the knowledge that helps you make better, more strategic organic content. Let's break down both sides of it, starting with culture:

The "culture" side of "platforms and culture" can help you define your cohorts, make relevant creative for them, and help inform your platform strategy. When I say culture, I don't just mean what's popular and trending now in the urban hip-hop world or what the "kids are into." I mean, do you know how to speak to the narrow cohorts you're trying to reach? Do you know how to speak to, say, 40–47-year-old men living in the Midwest who like hunting and fishing? Do you know what trends they're paying attention to? Do you know their common behaviors as consumers? Do you know how to get them to care about what you're selling?

If you were running a billboard ad campaign, this would mean paying attention to what's happening in the town you're in, and seeing how you can incorporate those nuances into the ad. In the world of 1950s, 1960s, and 1970s TV commercials, that meant paying attention to broad consumer interests (such as baseball) and incorporating those references in the commercial. On social, since we can make a high volume of content for low (or zero) cost for a variety of different cohorts, we need to have a nuanced understanding of what they're all paying attention to in culture.

People often misunderstand this—staying in tune with culture doesn't mean you need to dance on TikTok. If you're a B2B IT hardware company, you don't necessarily have to force a Drake reference into your content (or you could; I'm weirdly into that sort of thing as a tactic to experiment with). It's more about understanding what's culturally relevant to your target audience. Maybe it's an old TV show they grew up watching in the 1980s or '90s. Maybe it's tennis or golf or a hobby they've picked up. Maybe it's a consumer behavior trend in your industry. Or maybe it is a trending meme or a pop culture reference that's circulating around the internet.

By the way, one observation I see among some well-intentioned marketers and businesspeople is that they think the people who can make content relevant to a specific cohort are the people who look like the consumer cohorts. I don't think that's necessarily true. I don't think a forty-year-old woman is the only type of person who knows how to sell to other forty-year-old women. Similarly, I don't think twenty-two-year-olds are necessarily "better" at social media strategy than fifty-year-olds just because they "grew up with it." I understand these points of view, but I hope you consider this alternative perspective—especially if you're looking to build your own marketing team.

To gain insight into culture, you must pay attention to what I call "signals." Signals are any data points or information that give an indication of what's relevant to different consumer groups. Signals could take many forms, including:

- A consumer behavior or statistic
- Something a celebrity did
- Something an influencer did within cohorts you're looking at
- News articles
- Emerging trends on advertising platforms or sites like Google Trends
- Tweets, articles, or other content that sparks debate

◗ Research statistics about relevant topics

◗ Historic events

And much, much, much more.

For example, as I'm writing this there's a TikTok trend where people refer to "canon events," inspired by the film *Spider-Man: Across the Spider-Verse*. Canon events refer to moments that everyone has to experience for themselves to build character or learn a life lesson. Here's an example from a creator:

In this case, if you came across this trend, you could use it as an opportunity to showcase how well you understand your cohorts. What are the key life events for the people you're trying to reach? What are the most common behaviors that people can relate to? Can you weave in your product or service in a way that's authentic?

Another cultural observation you might have noticed based on news articles is that there's a growing number of

people doing flexible gig work. As work moves beyond nine-to-five for a lot of people, they may have more time during the day to browse social. You could use that data point to try out different platform strategies—maybe it's a sign that people have more time throughout the day, which means you could try posting at midday times like 10 a.m.–2 p.m. and compare that to other time slots.

As we'll cover more in the Post-Creative Strategy section, you might find trending memes, videos, or audio on various platforms that you can adapt into your content when you're scrolling through content yourself. Here's a physical therapist who layered on his own messaging over a popular video of hambone artist Steve Hickman. The video received 26.5 million views, at the time of writing.

Notice how the headline of the text here directly calls out a cohort, people over thirty who are starting to feel the effects of their lifestyle on their bodies:

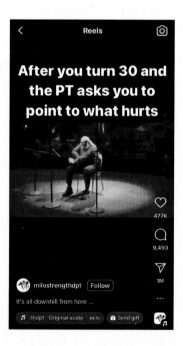

Adding titles that speak directly to your cohort group and calls them out literally is a good way to capture attention and make it relevant in the first few seconds.

By the way, when layering your content over memes, remember two things: 1) Give credit to the original poster in the copy (or the person featured in the video) to the best of your ability, and 2) layer on your own branding over the video so that when it's shared, viewers have a way to associate the message to your brand. This could be your logo, your own reaction (in the form of a TikTok duet or Instagram Remix), something else.

When you're looking into cultural trends, think of authentic ways that your brand can cross over and participate. Wendy's did a good job here with showcasing a photo of their Strawberry Frosty and calling it "Straw Barbie Frosty" in the copy of the tweet, given all the hype around Barbie in summer 2023 (see right).

If you're a B2B organization or an executive, you can pay attention to news trends in your industry or current events related to your area of expertise that you can talk about. You can use platforms to gather these events too—for example, you can tap into LinkedIn's suggested

searches to see what people are searching on the platform, and their "news" section to see what people on the platform are talking about that could be relevant to your field.

A lot of executives, service providers, and others are sometimes scared to tap into cultural trends or make content in general because they don't want their clients to take them less seriously. Many are worried about coming off as too "gimmicky," "cringey," or like "just another content creator" if they start using trending creative formats.

I'm passionate about this, because I personally have gone in directions with my personal content that others have been skeptical about. People have looked at me over the years and wondered, "Why is he talking about that?" "Why is he putting out content about this?" People wonder if I'm hurting myself somehow by speaking about certain subject matters.

The reality is, unless you're talking about something highly polarizing, most people don't give a crap. You may think you look silly by using a meme, a trending TikTok audio, or the "green screen" feature on platforms with you talking over an article screenshot in the background. But most viewers don't think of it that way.

The number of people who will consume your culturally relevant content and think, "I don't want to work with them," is a very small percentage. On the flip side, people who would've otherwise never considered working with your law firm, your dentistry, or your nursery now consider it because you were more human. For every 1 percent of people who don't want to work with you after watching your video, maybe 5 percent will work with you, and by putting more

culturally relevant content out you're giving yourself 4 percent more opportunity. What most professionals have wrong is that they think 80 percent of people will never work with them again, for every 1 percent of opportunity they might get.

But here's an important note: If you're not funny by nature, don't force it. If you aren't chill and casual, don't force it. This is a game of authenticity. If you're actually uptight and super polished, then maybe you need to stay in that zone because this strategy will leave you vulnerable if you do it from a place of inauthenticity.

Also, if you're authentically yourself, there are plenty of viewers who enjoy authentic stiff people or authentically awkward people. In fact, authentic awkward interviewers are emerging in social media as I'm writing this book.

On a similar note, I often hear from music artists who are aware about the potential of TikTok and other platforms, but they don't want to compromise on their authenticity or creativity just to get more views. They're worried that playing into trends may compromise who they are, their artistic style, and what got them to their current level in the first place.

If that's you, let me say it again: You don't need to compromise, nor do you need to make for trends and algorithms if you feel like that's not "you." Want to know why I say that? Because that's what I do. If you go look at my content on TikTok, I'm not dancing or playing into trends 24/7. What I do is put out content at scale every single day across all platforms on topics I want to be talking about, and things I'm passionate about.

That said, I'm always keeping an eye on trends and finding authentic places where I feel comfortable integrating them into my day-to-day content. I continue to challenge myself to be better at that.

For the artists in the scenario above, even though you don't need to compromise, realize you can't exist in a 2024 world and beyond while thinking that the "music is going to speak for itself." Record companies and audiences alike are looking for artists on social networks. It is what it is. You can be mad about it—guess what, there were artists who were mad that *TRL* was the most important platform. There were artists who were mad that disc jockeys in certain radio stations were the most important. The reality is, there are always platforms of the time that bring the most exposure for

commercial success. If you're an artist or a creative person, that's good news: Social networks are the most merit-based system ever. The DJ doesn't have to like you, the executives at MTV don't have to like you, Carson Daly doesn't have to like you; the world just has to like you.

But sitting at home and hoping that you can just put out music on Spotify and SoundCloud and call it a day is just not the reality of the record business in the modern world.

Ask yourself if leaning into cultural trends is truly inauthentic for you, or if you're just scared to go there from an insecurity standpoint. You need to challenge yourself to put the concepts from this book into practice while being authentic—that applies to everyone from content creators to small businesses to large brands.

There was a time when brands used to drive culture through their ads—in the days when people watched TV commercials at scale, Nike's "Just Do It" and Wendy's "Where's the Beef?" ad from 1984 were memorable, culture-defining moments. Today, it rarely happens. Of course, some of the biggest brands in the world manage to drive culture through widely used products. LVMH and Apple have products that play a key role in many people's lives and even their identities. Occasionally brands will drive culture through a properly executed activation at an event like the Formula 1 Miami Grand Prix. But brands rarely drive culture through their advertising because most ads feel like bland TV commercials, even when they're posted on social media. So, consumers scroll past them.

Today, in the new social media world, brands can drive culture not only through relevant content, but also through collaborations and even developing unique collectible products.

How would a brand go about driving culture through collectible items? Here's an example:

Start by looking at your cohorts. Who are you trying to reach? If you're trying to reach 16–20-year-old young males to buy your product, have you thought about signing a deal with the most famous Twitch gamers to create their rookie cards? If you made a set of cards similar to what Capri Sun did with Nickelodeon in 1991 and 1992 (clearly with the goal of building relevance for their Capri Sun juice), and put them into your product

packaging, you'd increase the likelihood that fans of those Twitch gamers would buy your product. You'd also broaden the product's appeal to collectors who want to buy cards of famous cultural figures today—these are individuals who may buy your product just to get the cards, use your product as a result, and purchase more later because they became fans of the product itself. Start with cohorts. Understand the cultural trends that cohort is paying attention to. Make a related collectible. That could be a sneaker collaboration, a collectible toy, a one-off comic book, a collectible pin, a magnet, a key chain, or even a digital collectible like a non-fungible token (NFT).

Now that I've talked a bit about the culture side of PAC, let's get into the P: platforms.

When you gain platform knowledge, you become aware of the variety of different features that exist across TikTok, YouTube, Facebook, LinkedIn, Instagram, Snapchat, and X (Twitter). You also get to know how to use the different features to create more awareness, engagement, and, ultimately, sales.

For example, Facebook allows users to upload photos as replies in the comments section. Using that observation, maybe you could add CTAs (calls-to-action) in your copy on Facebook Reels, asking people to leave their own photos in the comments and build a more intimate community. When people leave a comment or engage with your post, it's a sign to the platform that people like watching or interacting with your content; since the platform wants to keep people on for longer, it's more likely that your posts will be shown to them more often in the future (or to other groups of people who may also be interested in watching). It could also be an opportunity to get user-generated content that you repost in a different format, such as resharing those images on your Facebook and Instagram stories with your message layered on top of it.

Here's how a creator generated photo replies in Facebook Reels comments using a combination of in-app music and strong text call-to-action on the video:

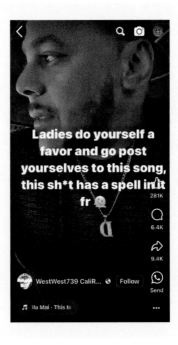

Another way to uncover popular creative formats is by paying attention to what the platform is prompting you to do. When scrolling on a platform, you might see a screen like this, prompting you to use a particular feature or try a new creative format:

Appeared in Instagram Reels tab in July 2023.

The above prompt appeared while scrolling on the Instagram Reels tab (Instagram's version of TikTok's For You page). It refers to the "Add Yours"

sticker—a sticker through which users can add their own videos or pictures that relate to different generic prompts. When clicking on "more prompts" in the screen, this is what we see:

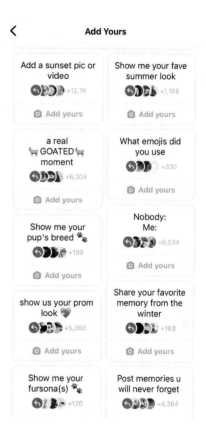

If you're scrolling and you see something like that, you could come up with a number of different hypotheses: Maybe Instagram wants more people to use the

"Add Yours" sticker. Maybe Instagram will reward accounts who use that sticker with more reach and awareness. Maybe it's an indicator that they want people to use other in-app creative features.

Whether those hypotheses end up being right or wrong, it would be a smart idea to experiment with it yourself.

When you scroll through your TikTok feed, you might notice some videos that have the words "CapCut: Try this template" above the username (at the time of writing). As you begin to see more and more of these videos, you should think about why they're being surfaced more often. If you do more research, you'd find that TikTok and CapCut (a video editing app) are both owned by the same parent company, and they've been integrated with each other. CapCut can help users create content with more speed and less overwhelm. As TikTok wants more users to create content on the platform, it makes sense that they might surface more videos created using CapCut; if you were to use CapCut templates in your TikTok videos, it might help your video's distribution. This is the thought process that's required.

Here are a few points to keep in mind to help you gain platform knowledge:

1. Take account of all the features a platform has.

At the most basic level, do you understand that you can duet and stitch videos on TikTok? Do you know that YouTube comments can link directly to a time stamp in the video? Do you know how long an Instagram Reel can be compared to a Spotlight Snap? Spend the time to play with each platform and see all that you can do.

2. Remember, the platform just wants you to stay on for longer.

Every platform just wants to keep users on for longer, which is the ultimate goal of all these features and updates. When you make content that people want to watch, consume, and engage with, you'll be rewarded with more reach. If you post a two-hour podcast interview on YouTube, it could still get a substantial amount of views and engagement for your business if that content is engaging enough. On the flip side, a short, five-second video with long, engaging text placed over it might also overindex in distribution if people are watching the video multiple times just to finish reading the text (signaling to the platform that the content might be good if people are watching repeatedly).

This is why there's no standard right answer to how long your content should be. It only matters whether people want to watch it. Sometimes people who are new to making content will think that they're "shadow-banned" by the platform if they aren't getting a lot of views—but more often than not, their content just isn't good enough, so the platform doesn't serve it to more people.

3. Pay attention to what is unique.

What kinds of features does a platform have that few to no other platforms have? For example, no other platform in this book besides Instagram lets users pin up to three comments in the comments section, at the time of writing. Also, at the time of writing, when users swipe past the last slide of a TikTok carousel in the For You page, it leads to the poster's profile—which is different from how Instagram carousels work (they don't allow users to swipe past the last tile). Pay attention to features on a platform that you don't see anywhere else—this can help inform what your content ideation should look like. For example, maybe the call-to-action on the last tile of your Instagram carousel would be to leave a comment or share this with a friend, but on TikTok you could try a "swipe and follow me" CTA and see if that works.

4. Pay attention to what's similar across platforms.

At the time of writing, all the platforms in this book besides LinkedIn already have some version of their own video feed like TikTok's For You page. YouTube, TikTok, LinkedIn, X (Twitter), and Instagram all have a scrubbing feature so users can fast-forward into the video (Facebook currently only has it for long-form videos, not Reels). Platform similarities can also give an indication to what their goals are, where they might be headed, and what behaviors they may or may not be trying to incentivize. You might be able to even implement similar tactics across platforms if you know where the similarities are.

For example, 81st Street Deli does a great job of showcasing their viral TikTok videos as pinned posts on their profile, but there's a missed opportunity in doing the same on Instagram (see next page).

On TikTok, their pinned videos feature trending food items from their menu—that way, when users land on their profile,

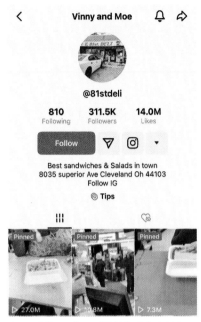

@81stdeli profile on TikTok, July 2023.

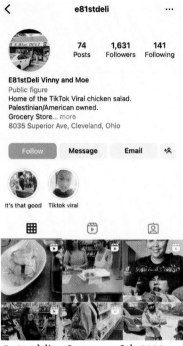

@e81stdeli on Instagram, July 2023.

they'll immediately see what they're known for.

However, Instagram also allows profiles to select pinned posts at the top. They could potentially pin some of those same videos (assuming they were posted contextually as Instagram Reels) or create a separate video "manifesto" of what their business is about and what content people can expect to find on the page. Another opportunity here is adding one or more links to their Instagram bio that point to areas they want to drive traf-fic to and utilizing Instagram's unique "Highlights" feature. Using Highlights, they could feature popular menu items, comments, or videos from their community about those items, or the interior of their deli, to give people a more thorough overview of who they are.

5. Notice how similar user behaviors show up differently on different platforms.

On LinkedIn, when a user likes or comments on a post, it will resurface the post on their connections' and followers' feeds. When a user likes or comments on an Instagram post, it doesn't directly show up in their followers' feeds again in the same way. These kinds of differences will impact how you make and distribute content. For example, maybe you could put an extra focus on creating business- or career-related discussions in your comments section on LinkedIn, given the greater distribution that comments will get you.

6. Stay up-to-date on new tests that platforms are running.

Platforms are always testing new features. Currently, YouTube is testing an AI-powered multilanguage voice-over dubbing tool. There are indications that other platforms are testing versions of AI chatbots and related features. Paying attention to these tests might give you an indication of the direction they're heading in.

7. Consider the psychology of the user when they're on the platform.

LinkedIn started out as a job search tool many years ago and still carries

that DNA—when people are browsing through LinkedIn, they're in a business and career state of mind. When those same people are browsing Facebook, they might be in the mindset of seeing what their high school and college friends are up to. When they're scrolling through TikTok, they might be in a lighthearted, casual mood. Each platform has its own context, which impacts how the piece of content is being consumed.

8. Be a practitioner, not a headline reader.

My plea is for you to *do* social media, not just read about it. Whether you're a twenty-two-year-old creator trying to build a brand around yourself, whether you're a fifty-two-year-old owner of a small business in your town, or an executive at a corporation—you have to be the practitioner. The only way to get good at this stuff is to make content, post it, and learn from it.

As you're playing around with various platforms and taking account of what features and creative units they have, you can reference this broad overview across platforms, at the time of writing:

Key Creative Units Across Platforms (at the time of writing)

	TikTok	Instagram	Facebook	YouTube	X	Snapchat	in personal profile	in company pages
Stories	✓	✓	✓			✓		
Multi-image assets	✓	✓	✓	✓	✓		✓	✓
Videos	✓	✓	✓	✓	✓	✓	✓	✓
Live	✓	✓	✓	✓	✓		✓	✓
In-app content creation features	✓	✓	✓	✓	✓	✓	✓	✓
Text-only posts	Native text-based videos	In stories	✓	✓	✓		✓	✓
GIFs		✓	via GIPHY	✓	via GIPHY	✓	✓	✓
Polls	✓	In stories and comments	✓	✓	✓	✓	✓	✓
Document uploads (PDFs)							✓	✓
Audio events					✓		✓	✓
Advertising capabilities	✓	✓	✓	✓	✓	✓	✓	✓

Some details in the previous chart might still be the same at the time you're reading this, and some platforms may have added new features and things may have changed. My hope is that you use the prior chart as a guide on the kinds of things you should be noticing as you're playing with different platforms and use that knowledge to inform how you make your strategic organic content.

Now it's your turn. Take your own time to audit each platform at the time you're reading this and fill out the following chart with a pen or marker. Can you figure out what each platform's current features and capabilities are?

Worksheet: Fill this out on your own								
	♪ (TikTok)	(Instagram)	f	▶ (YouTube)	X	(Snapchat)	**in** personal profile	**in** company pages
Ability to share content via private messages								
Ability to share in-feed posts dierctly to stories								
Collaborative posts (between 2 or more accounts)								
Tagging location on a post								
Video Live								
Live video feed								
Ability to add guests on the live								
Pinned comments on live stream								
Live stream remains in-feed after it's over								
Ability to create live events natively in-app								
Carousels								
Adding audio to carousels								
Ability to share >10 images								
Ability to tag people on each tile								
Natively sharing each tile to stories								
Ability to add both images & videos to carousels								
Sending carousels in DMs								

Worksheet: Fill this out on your own

	TikTok	Instagram	Facebook	YouTube	X	Snapchat	in personal profile	in company pages
Stand-alone Images								
Ability to add audio to images								
Ability to tag people on an image (not including tags in captions)								
Ability to add links onto in-feed images								
Videos								
Ability to post short-form videos that also surface in a separate, "For You-page style" feed (<60-sec)								
Ability to post long-form videos (>60-sec)								
Ability to add audio to videos natively in-app								
Ability to tag people on a video (not including tags in captions)								
Ability to add links directly onto videos								
Ability to record a video alongside another (i.e. duets on TikTok)								
Ability to record a video following a short snippet of another video (i.e. stitch on TikTok)								
Adding polls on videos								
Natively adding text and/or captions								
Natively adding stickers, emojis, and/or GIFs on videos								
Upload separate thumbnails to videos								

Worksheet: Fill this out on your own

Stories	♪ (TikTok)	◉ (Instagram)	f (Facebook)	▶ (YouTube)	X	👻 (Snapchat)	in personal profile	in company pages
Adding links								
Adding polls								
Adding product tags (for native shops)								
Adding lyrics to music on stories								
Natively adding stickers, emojis, and/or GIFs on stories								
Asking questions natively on stories								
Sharing tweets to stories								
Ability to record with native filters or lenses								

Strategic Organic Content (SOC): What Good Modern Advertising Looks Like

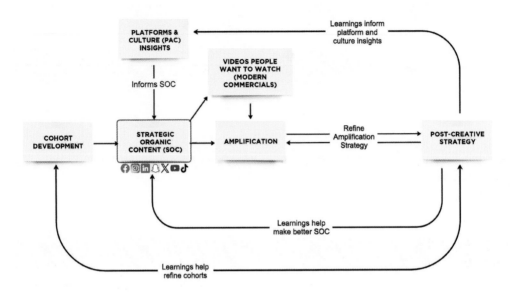

Over the next decade, the best communicators in the world will be the ones who are most talented at understanding how platforms work and understanding cultural nuances of hundreds of different consumer segmentations. PAC is the foundation of that, and SOC helps put PAC knowledge into practice.

Strategic organic content is meant to build brand, grow community, and create relevance. In the current social media landscape, it refers to the organic content that you post across Facebook, Instagram, LinkedIn, Snapchat, X (Twitter), YouTube, and TikTok.

It's a framework for how to make creative that people *want* to consume—the concept applies across many forms of advertising. Advertisers on television, radio, and outdoor media also have to know what "strategic" content looks like in those mediums. Advertisers have to know what the first few seconds of their commercial should look like and sound like so that you turn around from doing the dishes and look at the television. They have to know what a call-to-action should sound like on a radio ad that people can remember as they're driving. The same concepts apply on social media; it just so happens that with the number of social platforms that exist today, there are far more variables to consider when making strategic organic content compared to a strategic billboard or a strategic television commercial.

The bottom line is, being a good advertiser on social media is harder than being a good advertiser in the traditional marketing world. This is the biggest thing that Fortune 500 companies have upside down.

Often when I look at internal teams at brands and small businesses across the board, I notice some are "going through the motions" with their social media content. Some direct-to-consumer* brands blindly want to be sales-oriented, and so that's the way they approach their creative. Other times, small business owners just delegate their social media strategy to their twenty-two-year-old niece or nephew and the owners themselves aren't evaluating it (or don't know how). Fortune 500 brands will often enforce their brand guidelines on every piece of content, which makes their content less interesting and less relevant in many cases. They tend to bring television, print, and outdoor advertising mindsets to social media platforms.

That's why I put the *S* in SOC. Your content must be strategic. If you want to build brand and grow sales, you can't just post content for the sake of posting it.

Using your cultural insights and platform knowledge, SOC is about knowing how to make content specific for LinkedIn versus Facebook versus TikTok versus every other platform. How should your videos look on each platform? What should your images and carousels look like? What trending audio should you attach to your videos to increase watch time and shareability? What time should you post? How much copy should support it? What does the thumbnail look like? What do the first three seconds look and sound like? How do you incentivize people to hit the share button on a platform to create more awareness? SOC and PAC are about practicing creative and platform strategy at a "PhD" level.

When done properly, SOC helps you do a few things:

---

* Refers to brands that sell their products to consumers (usually online), without going through retailers or traditional "middlemen."

I. You build brand and relevance from day one.

When I talk about posting a high volume of content, one of the biggest misconceptions that people have is that I'm asking them to "spray and pray," "test and learn," or "throw stuff against the wall and see what sticks." While I absolutely believe in learning from what you post, I don't love phrases like "test and learn" because it undervalues the power of SOC. It leads some brands to treat social media as less valuable than other forms of marketing. I prefer to think about SOC as "marketing for the sake of better marketing." You post relevant content for your specific cohorts that can build brand on their own, but with the learnings you get from producing at a high volume, you're able to do even better marketing through your future content. That includes learnings from quantitative data and analytics, but also qualitative data from comments section insights.

I don't want you to try to build your business based off the "lightning bolt model"—in other words, don't spend all your time and resources on one piece of content trying to get it "right" and hoping to strike gold. Instead, try to put out four or five social media posts across each platform every day to give yourself more chances to have something hit.

The more content you're able to put out, the better. If you're trying to get better at tennis, practicing five days a week will improve your game more than if you practiced once a week. Each piece of content will help inform and refine your broader strategy.

This is why I always tell people to hold off on saying their strategy "isn't working" until they've been putting out content for 50–100 days. You can't just post four times on YouTube and give up because your Shorts got twenty views each.

When you're more relevant, then you'll be on top of mind for your customers or clients when they need what you're selling—this helps your sales-focused paid advertising campaigns convert more effectively at lower cost. With the way algorithms work now, relevance impacts reach; if your content is contextual and relevant to a specific cohort, then the platform will surface that content to more people within that cohort (as well as others outside the cohort who also may be interested).

The immediate goal with SOC isn't always sales, although some of your content may be more focused around your product or service than others. You'd be surprised how SOC can drive sales on its own (and definitely will help inform what your actual paid advertising campaigns should look like).

2. You can turn your best-performing content into performance ads to drive sales.

With the TikTokification of social media, every platform is moving in the direction of the interest graph—which means your content might get seventeen views if it doesn't resonate, but if it does, it might get one million regardless of the number of followers you have. If you have a piece of strategic organic content that overperforms compared to the average on your account, you have proof that people resonate with it. Then you can take the piece of content and tweak it a little. If you're a personal trainer and you have an Instagram reel that overperformed, you could tweak your copy to say something like "If you're interested in personal training in [your city], please email me at [your email]"—and run it as an Instagram ad within a five-mile radius of your town. This way, you mitigate the risk on your

paid advertising by using content that's already been proven to work through natural social media algorithms.

3. You can make higher-production commercials with proven insights.

When brands and agencies do advertising research, it usually comes in the forms of focus groups or studying industry research reports. With the volume of content that can be put out across platforms, we can gather research data points at a higher rate than ever before. Instead of using a series of small focus groups to guess what kind of commercial we should spend hundreds of thousands of dollars making, we can collect data from SOC and see what kinds of messaging resonates.

For example, Starbucks put out this tweet highlighting a relatable scenario for part of their customer base:

If this tweet did "well" compared to their average performance numbers or the quality of replies, Starbucks could decide to expand on it through short-form videos that they post across advertising platforms. For example, a quick search on TikTok along the same theme, "showing up late with coffee," pulls up a few short-form videos with titles like "pov: that employee that's always late but shows up with coffee," "me showing up to class 2 hours late with an iced coffee," "showing up late asf to work with a coffee," and more (see right).

Maybe they could combine their tweet theme with some of these video formats, and create some short videos titled "little miss shows up late to work with iced coffee" or "little miss shows up late to the family reunion with iced coffee" based on common scenarios people might find themselves in. If these clips happen to be broadly relatable, they could put even more resources behind this concept and turn it into a long-form, higher-production skit—maybe getting some influencers involved. By the time they decide to produce that skit and amplify it across channels like YouTube, OTT, CTV, or standard television commercials, they would have gathered data that proved consumers care about the message. They would've minimized the risk before in-

vesting those tens of thousands or hundreds of thousands of dollars.

This is how a simple post on X (Twitter) can be the seed that leads to a high-budget advertising campaign.

The more SOC you put out, the better insights you'll have—you'll get a sense for what content resonates, how to effectively use platform features, and you'll learn how to make your next piece of con-

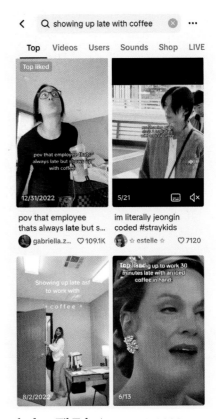

Searched on TikTok, August 23, 2023.

tent better than the one before it. There's no permanent right answer to what the "best practices" are on advertising platforms because things shift and change so much. That's why you should be posting as much as humanly possible—so you can uncover new learnings as they happen.

Consider the following points as you're making SOC for your personal brand, your business, your clients, or the company you're working for.

Does your content feel like an ad?

When companies think of what their LinkedIn posts should look like, many of them immediately go into a PR-driven mindset and default into promoting what their company is doing, instead of actually providing value. This post from Gong approaches things differently (see right).

Here, the first two lines in the copy immediately address the intended audience—"MENTAL HEALTH MATTERS. As a leader, it's part of your job to establish emotional stability." The headline of the image is "Mental health is a challenge for sellers"—so immediately this appeals to both leaders in organizations as well as some junior salespeople who might be brave enough to engage with the content, which means their managers might see it (given how LinkedIn's algorithm works).

The presentation of data in a graph-style format is also native to the psychology of the LinkedIn audience when they're on the platform—they're in a business, sales, and overall professional mindset. It's a visual piece of content that brings value by providing information without overly promoting the company—in fact, the company name is weaved into the graph in a subtle, smart way near the bottom.

The dimensions of the image also maximize the amount of space taken up

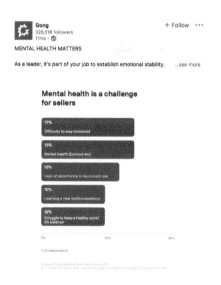

in the feed, which can help boost engagement in some cases.

When clicking "see more" and expanding on the text, this is what we see:

Here we see more details around the context of the graph, the stats, and tactical pieces of advice for leaders that are broken up in an easy-to-read format (again, providing value to their audience around a common topic many of them may be thinking about).

Some potential ways to improve might be the following: What about changing colors on the graph for easier readability? What about making the title larger on the graph? Could that catch more people as they're scrolling? What about adding a call-to-action at the end of the copy, or leaving the first comment from the company account (or an executive from the company) to create more engagement on the post? Would all of this result in greater reach?

The first two lines of the copy convey a strong point of view, but another way to approach it might be adding a "cliffhanger" at the end of line 2 that incentivizes readers to click the "see more" button on LinkedIn to expand the copy and continue reading to see what the point of view is.

If you're at a B2B company putting out content on LinkedIn, the best advice I have is to pretend that your company is the "B2B magazine" of your industry. Pretend your organization is the host of a show related to your subject matter on Sirius radio, and your goal is to get the best ratings. Instead of trying to promote your business in every post, make content that people in your cohort categories will be interested in consuming. The best part is, in the B2B world, you don't need hundreds of thousands of views on your content. If you're making content for decision makers in the IT sector, maybe a couple hundred views from people in those roles is enough to generate return on investment.

A strategy I always recommend to B2B organizations or service providers is to invite your target decision makers to be guests on your podcast. This has a few benefits: 1) You'll be able to build relationships with potential customers that may lead to sales in the long term; 2) after six months of doing this, the potential customers that you'd normally reach out to will now be reaching out to you to get on your podcast; and 3) the podcast is content that you can post across platforms—you can cut up clips from that podcast, post it organically, and take the ones that perform well and run those as ads on LinkedIn against others from your target customer base.

What does the hook of your video look like?

The hook is the first thing that a user sees when they're scrolling, and they come across your content.

If you're posting a video, then the hook is everything that appears in the first three seconds or so. That includes the title, the thumbnail, any captions you might use, the opening lines, the character or person in the video, and the overall design and format of the post.

If you're posting an image, consider what colors are most prominent, what words are largest, and other elements that will catch the viewer's eye.

Out of all the variables, the hook is one of the most important ones because it dictates the first impression of your content. This is where you either catch people's attention or let them scroll past. Most of us don't sit on the couch anymore with the remote in our hands, bound by the *TV Guide* schedule with only a few channels to choose from. We live in a world where there are obnoxious amounts of information getting thrown at us—which means if you're not catching people's eyes in the first second or two, they're going to scroll to the next piece of content in their feed. The hook is the part where the audience decides if the piece of content is relevant to them or not.

Check out this TikTok video, for example:

There are multiple variables here that help create an engaging hook:

1. The green screen video effect: Green screen effect allows creators to add their commentary or reaction on top of either a picture or a video in the background. In this case, the creator used TikTok's native "duet" feature (which allows you to post your video in combination with another video from another account, in various formats) and selected "green screen" as the format for the duet. This means the video is playing in the background, with the creator's face in the corner providing their commentary over it.

This format helps create an eye-catching hook that makes viewers curious about what the creator is going to say.

I also think the green screen format is a great one because it allows people to comment over headlines, articles, and screenshots of other posts that may be relevant to what your consumers care about. It can be an easy way to make content; if you're a real estate professional, chances are you have some opinions about current interest rates or home-buying trends in your area. You could find a relevant article that talks about those things with an intriguing headline, and layer on a "green screen" with your opinion. If you want more distribution on special press releases and announcements your company makes, you can "green screen" it for extra distribution instead of just posting that content on your blog and letting it sit there.

2. Title and first three seconds of the video: The title "Where is the surgeon hiding?" along with the creator saying "Where is the surgeon?" out loud in the first few seconds of the video creates curiosity. Adding a title that asks a thought-provoking or interesting question like this might lead to more users staying on the video to find the answers.

   In this example, the readability of the title might be something to improve. The white text against the green background might not have been as readable as, say, using Tik-Tok's in-app features to add a black background behind the white text so it's a bit more readable. This is where things get subjective—just because you or I or someone in the organization likes a particular color doesn't

mean that color is the one that'll catch the most attention. In this scenario, maybe the creator could try multiple different colors in the headlines, post all the versions, and see which one actually ends up working the best.

In the first few frames of the video, there's also a slight pause before the creator starts talking. The first frame of the video appears as a static image, rather than immediately focusing on the main point of the video. The first few seconds of a video are too valuable to waste time with slow starts, or extra frames that aren't 100 percent necessary. It's best to get into the message as fast as possible; otherwise you'll lose viewers.

The first three seconds are critical to how relevant your video feels to your intended audience—this is the place to feature actors and actresses who look like the people you want to reach, add thought-provoking headlines, or add movement and camera angles that make people curious about what the video's going to say.

3. The sound: Native TikTok audio involving the *Mission: Impossible* theme song was added here and is playing in the background as the creator is talking. The familiarity of the song is a good way

to catch attention and help the distribution of the video; if TikTok sees that a lot of people are watching videos with that audio attached, then it's potentially more likely they'll give favorable distribution to other videos that have the same audio.

With certain platforms today, you also have the option to repost a piece of content with new edits, once you see how it does the first time around. You can change one variable—the title, the hook, or the overall video format, or anything else—then repost it and see how it does. This might work better on some platforms than others; sometimes, if your content is being shown predominantly to your follow-

ers, showing the same piece of content to them again within a short time frame (even with slight tweaks) might limit performance. Some platforms will show you what percentage of your viewers were followers versus nonfollowers, and you can use that data to inform your strategy here.

When it comes to video formats and styles, it's tempting for brands to keep the same style across their content to stay within their brand guidelines. For example, Athletic Greens had a smart strategy partnering with Dr. Andrew Huberman for a content series; however, these three thumbnails from their Instagram Reels all have a similar design:

Dr. Andrew Huberman on Resilience with AG1

Dr. Andrew Huberman More on Foundational Nutrition with AG1

Dr. Andrew Huberman on the Gut Microbiome with AG1

Athletic Greens Instagram thumbnails on three videos.

If they repeatedly used this format as part of their hook because of actual data that showed this design increased performance, then that's an appropriate strategy. However, a lot of brands tend to sacrifice performance, engagement, and relevance because they make what they want to make rather than what consumers want to see. Usually this means creating strict guidelines around things like logo placements, colors, how the product is used, and other things that the consumer doesn't care about.

Do people spend time watching and interacting with your content?

Today we have unparalleled access to data on how people are consuming our content. Back when I ran a full-page ad in the *New York Times* for Wine Library, I couldn't see exactly how many people saw it and actually consumed it. If a brand is running a TV commercial, they might have a guess for what the "potential reach" is, but they don't know how many people actually saw it and paid attention to it (unless they use creative attribution methods, like QR codes or special phone numbers as parts of their call-to-action).

Now every platform provides analytics on how people are consuming your content, and this quantitative data is an important part of your feedback loop to make even better content the next time around. If you post something on TikTok, you can get insights on average watch time, percentage of viewers who watched the full video, number of new followers you got from the piece of content, and more. This feedback lets you ask smart questions. Why is one piece of content getting more followers than another piece of content? Why are some of your videos getting more people to watch to the end? Is it the topic? Is it the creative format? Is it your copy that makes people watch? You might not be 100 percent sure on these answers, but that's okay—as long as you have a hypothesis, you can continue to try things.

At the time of writing, YouTube provides some of the most thorough analytics out of any platform in this book. You can see audience retention graphs for long-form videos on YouTube analytics, which can help you find out which moments in your long-form video that people are resonating with the most (based on which parts of the video got the most replays or shares).

Does your content evoke emotion and tell a story?

If you tell your story properly, your audience will be willing to sit down and pay attention to you for longer than they normally would. A common misconception is that your content has to be short to capture attention. The reality is, we live in a world where so many people binge-watch *Game of Thrones* or *Stranger Things* for hours and hours on the weekend. People will sit and have a Marvel movie marathon and spend the entire day watching films back-to-back. They'll also scroll past a thirty-second YouTube short if it's not engaging.

It's not about the length of your content; it's about how good your content is.

When you make content, make it for the person who is consuming it. Not for yourself. What you make needs to be either informative, thought-provoking, entertaining, or a mix of multiple different elements. Once you catch attention with a strong hook, are you keeping their attention throughout the length of your video? What's their incentive to watch till the thirty-second mark, the one-minute mark, or the three-minute mark?

Is your content native to the platform?

Once you have a sense for who you're making content for, you need to understand how to make content within the creative units. An important part of this is using each platform's features in a way that leverages their unique capabilities.

Think of it this way:

All of us act differently when we're in a boardroom versus when we're on a trip to Vegas with our closest friends. We act differently with our family than with our coworkers. Being "native to a platform" is no different than being aware of the context of the room that you're in.

You'd want to make your content "blend into" the platform as much as possible. If you were running ads on Hulu, you might think about how to make it similar to the show you're running ads on. If you're running radio ads, that would mean incorporating jingles and music similar to the radio station that you're running ads on.

Notice how Brit + Co* uses Instagram carousels to display a decision tree across multiple carousel tiles (see next page). The first tile asks a question and serves as the

---

* Full disclosure: I'm an investor.

"hook," enticing people to swipe based on their answer. The decision tree expands into many different options as users keep sliding and ends on a wholesome message. Notice that in the first tile, there's a little hint through the design of the image that there's a continuation in tile 2 and beyond. It reminds users that the post is a carousel and that there's more to swipe through, as sometimes in-feed graphics can be mistaken for stand-alone images as users are scrolling fast in-feed.

The carousel is also culturally relevant for the time it was posted (Mother's Day), and hits on a common emotion and pain point that certain people have around holidays when they have challenges with their family situation.

If this carousel performed worse than Brit + Co's usual numbers, they could tweak the format in the future by trying any number of things. For example, they could try designing an entire flowchart in one image instead of multiple (so that it can be quickly consumed at a glance instead of asking users to swipe through multiple tiles).

When you're making content native to a platform, there are a few elements to consider:

1. What sizes and dimensions are you working with?

For example, on Instagram, the snapshot of your video as it appears on your profile grid is only a portion of your full vertical video (at the time of writing). If you're reposting a TikTok video to Instagram, one of the tweaks you might make is adding a specially designed Instagram thumbnail as the first frame of your video

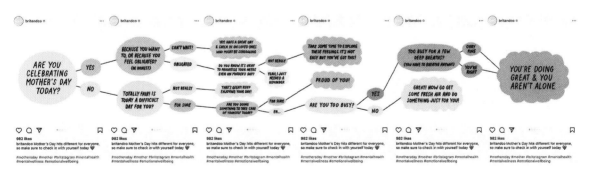

Brit + Co Instagram carousel.

where the key elements are all placed within the dimensions necessary to show up in your grid.

2. Are you using a platform's in-app features?

This is one of the easier ways to make your content native to a platform—if you're posting a video clip, you can use in-app features across platforms to add a title to your video. That way, the video leverages designs and features that are unique to the platform. Snapchat, for example, lets users add text to a thin black bar within the app—a format that's unique to the platform.

Instagram and TikTok both allow you to add polls on to your videos, for example, but the polls aren't designed in the same way. Every platform has a number of these in-app features that make them different from the others.

3. Does your copy reference contextual elements from the platform?

People tend to overlook the importance of copy when making content, but this is where you have the opportunity to address your viewers directly. You could say things like "Hey Instagram" or "Hey Facebook" at the beginning of your copy to call out the users, or reference specific calls-to-action. On Instagram, you'd say "share this with your friends," but on LinkedIn, you'd say "send this to a colleague" (since that's what LinkedIn calls their share feature at the time of writing this). On Instagram, you'd say "save this post," but on X (Twitter) you'd say "bookmark this." If you're using your own audio on a Facebook or Instagram reel that feels inspirational, funny, motivational, or any other kind of audio that people can add to their own Reels, you can say something like "make a reel using this audio" in the copy.

4. Are you using cultural trends within each platform?

Chipotle in this example repurposed a TikTok to an Instagram Reel (see next page).

It was the same video with the same copy, but the trending sound they used in the background of this short looping video was different on each platform.

I often get asked whether it's okay to post the exact same piece of content across multiple platforms to increase output and save time. I don't love this approach because people use it as an excuse to "copy and paste" creative across platforms without any thought. There are too many contextual nuances from platform to platform, and blind copying and pasting means you're leaving opportunity for relevance and distribution on the table. There are always small tweaks you can make—even if it's just in the copy or the audio you use. My team does have a content repurposing strategy where we'll sometimes take the same piece of content and distribute it across multiple platforms. But I know that if I made a video specifically for Facebook it would perform better than something that was repurposed from somewhere else.

Are you putting out enough volume of content?

Two partners walked up to me at VeeCon 2023 and told me, "We want to change the world."

I loved it—I said, "Good!" After exchanging some warm feelings and shaking hands, I asked them how many times they were posting content.

They told me they were really working

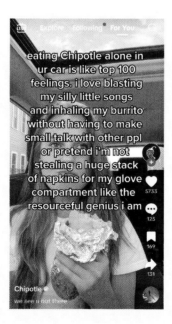

hard, and they added another person to their team. I pushed back: "How much content are you putting out?"

They replied, "Not enough."

For the third time, I asked again, "How much content are you putting out?"

Eventually, they told me the truth: They were publishing one post a week.

I have a lot of love for those two and I love every business owner, creator, or leader who has big ambitions. I hear from a lot of entrepreneurs and business owners who aspire to be billionaires, or artists who aspire to be the next Drake. When I ask about how much content they're putting out to bring awareness around their mission, the answer is almost always too little.

With those two who walked up to me at VeeCon, I pulled out my phone and filmed a piece of content with them right then and there, prompting them to talk about some of the key points around what they know. You can watch the interaction at garyvee.com/quitoverthinking. I think it'll help a lot of you.

People always get into the "quality" versus "quantity" debate when it comes to content. To me, the answer is always both. But putting out more quantity is what gives you an indication to what

quality actually is. The more formats you put out, the more consumer segmentations you make content for, the more insights you get on what's resonating. Does a short looping video perform better on X (Twitter) than a GIF of the same looping video? Does a status update on LinkedIn perform better than putting the same quote in a native "template" in-app, making it appear more like a graphic? What platform drives the most link clicks for you when you link to an external URL?

You won't know answers to these questions unless you're posting a variety of different types of content across platforms at a high volume. Even though I believe creative quality is the variable of success, it's the quantity execution that's the opportunity to figure out what quality is.

And no, you're not "oversaturating" the feed or annoying people by posting more. Most of your content isn't even being seen because of the number of apps out there, and the number of distractions available in everybody's day-to-day life.

Some people make the mistake of thinking that their content will perform better if they post less. If that's you, I would challenge you to take a deeper look at the numbers. In many cases, people might get, say, 1,000 views on a post if you're posting once a day, and that might drop down to 500 per post when they're posting four times a day. But even though your reach per post is lower, you're still getting a total of 2,000 views per day versus 1,000 views per day with your higher quantity. The results might differ based on the platform, but make sure you measure it instead of guessing.

Bottom line? Post more.

Is your copy optimized for the platform?

As people increasingly use platforms like TikTok and Instagram as search engines, the copy (the caption) on your post plays a huge role. The creator of the following video received 12.9 million views (at the time of writing); it's an eleven-second video that starts with "pov: you're feeling lazy and don't feel like doing anything" (which is relatable for a large group of people) and ends with a CTA to "read the caption," where there's longer copy elaborating on a solution to the problem.

If done right, your copy can be the primary driver of your content's distribution. Your copy can be a place where you add additional context around your piece of content and build on it further. You could

reference the cohorts you're trying to reach by starting with a line like "For all the dads out there" or add a curiosity-provoking line that keeps people watching until the end.

Platforms across the board continue to expand the character limits for copy at the time of writing, which is a sign that they appreciate the greater length and the value it adds to the content. If you're a strong writer, you could take advantage of text-only posts on Facebook and LinkedIn, long-form posts on X (Twitter), YouTube Community tab posts, and maxing out the character limits on Instagram and TikTok.

What does your profile hygiene look like?

Before you start posting content it's important to make sure that your profile is set up in the right way, so that when viewers click through to your profile after watching your video, they know exactly who you are and what you do.

For example, ATL Mixers did a great job with this TikTok video on the next page; they used catchy audio in the background, and they showed the process of making a summer drink (a topic that would be top of mind for people in July, when this was posted). Videos that show the process of making something—a drink, a recipe, or a special kind of food—are interesting for people to watch because they want to see the outcome.

In this case, ATL Mixers got 19.9 million views on this video at the time of writing. However, the link in bio doesn't go to their website; it goes to their Instagram page.

On their Instagram page, they have a short bio explaining what they do and Instagram highlights featuring a couple of client reviews, but they don't have a website link there in bio or a phone number.

If someone wanted to hire them for a private event, what would they do? Sign up on a website? Message them on Instagram? There's no obvious call-to-action on what to do, and there were undoubtedly some TikTok viewers who would've hired them if the steps were clearer. A better strategy would've been to link to a website in their TikTok bio with a form to fill out or a phone number to call. They could do the same on their Instagram page, in addition to using the Highlights feature to showcase other parts of their business, such as footage from events they've done in the past or short videos of top drink recipes.

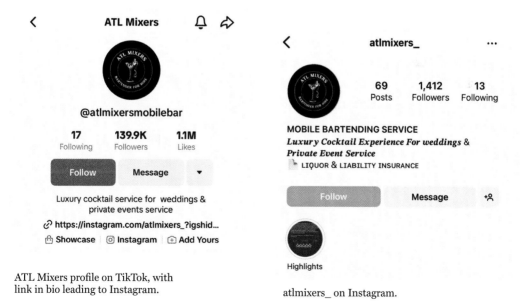

ATL Mixers profile on TikTok, with
link in bio leading to Instagram.

atlmixers_ on Instagram.

This is just a classic example of missed opportunities when you don't optimize every angle. The reason this book is going so deep is that there are so many little details that make up the full picture. I couldn't even explain to you the potential revenue loss that ATL Mixers missed out on by not maximizing their profile during this viral moment.

You should make sure that people can easily see who you are, what you do, and have the chance to take an action (whether it's clicking a link to your website, calling your number, or any other important action you want people to take). It's our job as operators to eliminate friction for users who want to do things with us.

Are you showing different sides of yourself, your brand, or your business?

I often notice businesspeople post a lot of technical how-to videos related to their products or services, but don't share as much about themselves. You don't need to share more than what you're comfortable with—I rarely talk about my personal life in my content and everyone is in control of how open or private they want to be.

However, you might completely change the trajectory of your business with one post about your experience as a stay-at-home parent. That might be the post that gets a ton of views because millions of other parents relate to it. Through that increased distribution, you could build awareness for your business, assuming your profile hygiene is on point, and build trust as a result of sharing your personal side. Your video about your passion for sneaker collecting might lead to more business for your B2B hardware company because your customers' kids who are in college or high school shared your videos with them. If you built up a following through posting your modeling photos on Instagram, but you love food, consider posting about your favorite recipes one out of every five posts.

One thing I'd ask all of you reading is, do you act differently around your friends than you act professionally? Do you act differently around your family than you act professionally? Consider bringing those versions of you to your business and to your content in general. This is something people have been told for a long time not to do, but I'm telling you that you should. I believe history will prove me, this book, and this concept to be right.

People are always worried about losing respect with their audience or posting something that no one cares about. The reality is, putting out content is never a bad thing. The more topics you touch on, the more opportunities you have to relate to people.

Do you occasionally mix in content to get answers to questions you have?

The best way to figure out what content to make is to literally ask the audience. You could use the poll feature (which multiple platforms have) to ask questions and gather data or use other creative units. For example, say you have a YouTube channel about fitness, but you really want to post about fashion and you're not sure how people will react. You could start by doing a poll through the YouTube Community tab, where you ask people, *"I'm really passionate about fashion and I have a lot of interesting tips to share, would you all be interested in seeing 1 or 2 videos?"* You could take it a step further and ask, *"Have you ever thought about dressing better? What's stopping you?"*

You could even state a strong point of view that you have on video related to your business and see if people have different takes in the comments. For ex-

ample, if you have a bike shop and you're wondering what bikes people are most interested in, you could make a video pointing to one and say, *"This bike is the best for mountain biking."* You might get some comments from people who disagree or have other recommendations, which would give you a sense for what's running through people's minds.

Those insights would then inform the ideation of your future content.

Are you finding the right balance between asking for business while providing value?

This is a concept I talked about in *Jab, Jab, Jab, Right Hook*, and it's still an important topic to consider to this day.

Back then, I noticed that people usually fell into one of two categories: They would either not put out enough "jabs" (free value) to balance out their "right hooks" (asking for business), or they would *only* put out free value and be too scared to ask for business.

There's no set formula here and every business and brand needs to find its own balance, but make sure you're doing both. As you're putting out free, valuable organic content across platforms, make sure you're taking the overperformers and turning them into sales-focused ads. Every now and then when you have something specific to promote, you can even post a sales-focused piece of content organically across platforms, directly asking people to buy or sign up.

If you're *only* asking people to buy, however, they'll quickly tune you out, so make sure to balance out those asks with a high volume of valuable content.

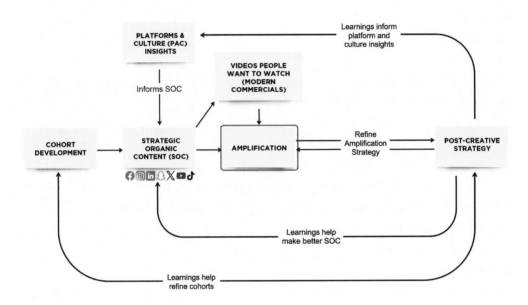

Amplification: Spending Against What Works, aka Not Wasting a Penny

The first television commercial aired in 1941 before a game between the Brooklyn Dodgers and Philadelphia Phillies. The company that ran it, Bulova watches, paid somewhere around $4 to $9 to air the commercial; according to an infla-tion calculator from the Federal Reserve Bank of Minneapolis, $9 in 1941 is just over $180 in 2023.[13] Incredibly cheap.

It featured a picture of a United States map, with a clock in the middle display-ing the company's name. A narrator in the background read out the words "America runs on Bulova time," and that was it. It was before people knew how to leverage the visual components of TV, and how to make commercials that were different from radio ads that ruled the day prior to television.

Yet, despite the lack of "SOC" and "PAC" understanding on what makes a great TV commercial, it was still a good deal for the time.

Similarly, over the last decade, brands and businesses were able to cover up mediocre content through the extreme underpriced nature of social media advertising.

Marketers would be able to set up a Facebook conversion campaign, write some copy, select a stock photo from their built-in library, and actually get results. The supply of quality ads was so low that businesses could get away with generic creative. It's like when you're the only restaurant in town—people are still going to eat your food even if it isn't excellent. When there are fifteen restaurants in town, you need to serve better food.

As more advertisers have come in, and as advertising platforms' algorithms have evolved, creative has become the most important variable to a successful media campaign. With Meta's Advantage+ shopping campaigns, you can feed up to 150 combinations of creative (at the time of writing) and the platform will automatically serve the creative to the best possible audiences to hit your ad objective. The targeting with Advantage+ shopping campaigns would be broad, limited only by age and the geographic area, and the algorithm would do the rest. The paid advertising ecosystem across platforms is moving in the same direction as their organic content algorithms: They're becoming more and more interest-graph led. The platforms (depending on their sophistication) will take your creative, and they'll distribute it to whoever is most likely to take the action you want them to take—whether it's visiting your website, buying your product, signing up with their email, or any other action-based ad objectives the platform offers.

At the time of writing, Facebook, Google Ads (which includes YouTube), Instagram, and TikTok are currently leading the way in terms of the sophistication of their advertising algorithm. For example, with Google's Performance Max campaign type, the algorithm is built to optimize performance in real time and find who's most likely to convert across all of Google's channels (like YouTube, Display, Search, Discover, Gmail, and Maps).

What does that mean for you? For instance, if you're looking to get donations for a nonprofit, you could run an ad campaign on Facebook, Instagram, TikTok, or YouTube, and layer on age, country, and interest-based targeting related to your category (on Facebook and Instagram, that might mean targeting people interested in health and wellness if you've got a nonprofit related to feeding people). You could rely on the platforms to find the best donors through their algorithms, without manually targeting 30–35-year-old high-income men and women in New York City who are interested in health and wellness. You might just target everyone in the US who is interested in health and wellness and see who converts.

However, there's still a place for setting narrower targeting based on the cohorts you're trying to reach. Not all platforms' algorithms are equally advanced in terms of automatically distributing your creative to the perfect audience, and some mediums work differently than others. If you're running podcast ads on Spotify, you wouldn't want to broadly target every podcast that exists because they don't

have an interest-graph-driven conversion algorithm that can automatically find listeners most likely to convert. In that case, you'd want to choose targeting categories based on your cohort strategy. Through platforms like Nextdoor (a hyperlocal social network) you might benefit from layering on zip code–specific targeting with creative that's contextual to local areas. X (Twitter) allows advertisers to target based on keywords people search in their search queries. Even on Facebook, YouTube, Instagram, and TikTok, layering on manual, narrow targeting can be beneficial sometimes— especially when you know for a fact that your creative resonates with that group through your organic content insights.

Your ad objective also plays a role—if you're optimizing for reach (showing your ads to as many people as possible in a target audience) rather than a specific action such as a website visit or a conversion, you might want to go narrower with your targeting or use your first-party data so that the platforms aren't showing your ad to completely random people.

If you're new to the world of paid advertising, experiment with everything; try a campaign where you manually specify targeting details that are related to cohorts who resonated with your organic creative and try some with broader targeting. There are a lot of nuances here when it comes to what your ad targeting should be, what a good cost per thousand impressions (CPM) is, what your maximum ad frequency should be, and more—the best way to learn is by running campaigns yourself.

By putting out SOC informed by PAC insights, you can minimize the risk of wasting money on your ad campaigns and unnecessarily driving up your customer acquisition cost (CAC). This is especially important in the modern world, after Apple's iOS 14.5 update, which introduced App Tracking Transparency (ATT). After this change, apps had to ask users for permission to track their activities across other apps and websites.

Since users had to opt in (rather than opt out), many chose not to opt in—this created challenges for advertisers as it limited the amount of data that advertising platforms had access to. A lot of direct-to-consumer and e-commerce businesses were built off running Facebook ads to their websites, and then retargeting those visitors over and over again until they converted. In a post–iOS 14.5 world, it became much harder for platforms like Facebook to track who landed on your website; the available data became far more limited. Even on desktop devices, there are more and more limitations on the data shared between browsers and advertising platforms. This has a couple of implications:

1. It's one of the reasons why platforms like Instagram and TikTok are focused on building out their own "Shops" that allow users to browse products and buy within the app itself. If users buy within the app, they own that data and they can use it to serve more relevant ads to people rather than being at the mercy of other companies like Apple. TikTok, for example, currently has a Shop Retargeting feature that allows advertisers to show ads to people who have interacted with their TikTok Shop.

2. Building brand through organic content is more imperative than ever. Today, the best way to reach high-intent audiences is through well-made content. Even in your ad campaigns, your creative is the most important variable because the algorithm generally does the job of delivering the content to the people most likely to watch or convert.

For example, let's say you're a plumber with $700 to spend on paid ads this month. You've been putting out content already across platforms for months, you're seeing some overperform organically, and you're trying to decide where to allocate your budget.

The first thing to do in this situation is find the normal range of views and engagements you get on your organic posts across platforms. If most of your posts get 5 to 25 views but seven of the videos got 500 to 700, then that's a clear "overindex" in performance, even if it's not "viral" by everyone else's standards.

Before running media, make sure to slightly tweak those seven videos visually to be more sales focused. If your video is funny, maybe you could add a few frames to the end of the video that say, "If you want a plumber with 12 years of experience and also a sense of humor, click here to get a free consultation." You could also add a version of that line to the copy of your video.

Then you can take those seven videos and spend $100 against each of them within a five-mile radius of your town. Look at which two performed the best and got you the most consultations, and next month spend more money on that

ad. You could also repurpose it for other platforms—if you ran the ad on Facebook initially, try adding a native title on the video using TikTok's content creation tools and try captioning it in the app. Then post it on TikTok and amplify it there if it does well organically.

The biggest mistake a lot of small businesses and service providers make in this situation is spending too much of their budget too quickly. With the approach above, you're giving yourself a chance to get more proof the ad works before investing more money in it.

If you have the resources, you can expand your winning ads into more broadly relatable videos that people want to watch (modern commercials) and run those as YouTube pre-roll ads.

YouTube is also exciting because it's a gateway into CTV ads for many. In fact, I had a fun moment with my dad at Cannes Lions 2023, when he was talking about a commercial that came on when he was "watching television" and how he couldn't hit the "skip ad" button fast enough. The fascinating insight here is, although he called it a television commercial, it was an ad on YouTube that he was watching on a connected TV device.

Three in four TV-owning households

had smart TVs (which can access the internet and streaming services and integrate with connected TV devices like Roku or Amazon Fire TV Stick) as of Q1 2023.[14]

Through CTV devices, people can watch YouTube, OTT streaming services like Hulu and Netflix, and FAST channels such as Tubi or Pluto TV.

Streaming services like Hulu and devices like Roku have increasingly accessible advertising options for small businesses. Even if you're a solopreneur, you can literally run ads on shows that play when people are watching something on Hulu. At the time of writing, if you get approved as a small-medium business on Hulu, you can run ads for as little as $500 per month. Just pause and think about that for a minute—opportunities like this used to be hundreds of thousands, or millions of dollars at minimum in the world of TV commercials. Now you can have a real "commercial" for your personal brand, your startup, your small local business during major shows on Hulu that people are actually watching.

These aren't just for brand awareness campaigns. For example, Roku partnered up with Shopify to let users buy products through their TVs when an ad plays, using the Roku remote. Through Roku's partnership with Instacart, CPG brands can see if people purchased their product on Instacart after seeing an ad on Roku.

As you get proficient at running ads on social media platforms, I believe those same skills will translate to advertising on OTT, FAST channels, and CTV. Media buying dynamics on streaming services are becoming increasingly similar to the marketplace bidding process on social networks.

Please note: This is important for those in the Fortune 500 landscape. The social media frameworks are eating up your beloved traditional media platforms. It's time to have the humility to lean into the reality of the post-2023 world.

In a sense, your paid ads strategy should be an extension of your organic content strategy—if you're not putting out strategic organic content regularly, then your ads won't be nearly as effective because you won't have any indications of what is resonating with people. You'll be guessing a lot more.

Whether you're amplifying creative on streaming services, social media, traditional TV commercials, or other channels, keep in mind that every ad channel can either be overpriced or underpriced. It depends on how you use it. Of course, some channels may be inherently underpriced or overpriced based on supply and demand. If you're running ads on platforms that are relatively early in their maturity, before there are a ton of other advertisers competing with you for the limited ad space, you're going to get more people consuming your ad for a cheaper cost. At the same time, if you're running an ad on Instagram with zero SOC principles that's not native at all to the platform, the results you get might lead you to believe that Instagram ads are overpriced.

Even channels that are traditionally overpriced could be underpriced for brands that know how to execute well.

For a lot of direct-to-consumer brands, television commercials can work when they're direct response focused. The more your ad looks like an infomercial, the more it could drive sales in a television commercial environment. The key is to make it direct response focused and geared toward getting more sign-ups and website visits, rather than brand awareness alone.

One way to approach this would be to create two versions of the same ad: one with a QR code on-screen at the end, and another with the website link. Compared to a website link, a QR code might be lower friction. Companies could run both ads through YouTube pre-roll to get a sense for which one results in the most website traffic, and amplify the winner through a broader OTT, CTV, and remnant television commercial campaign.

While informercial-style commercials would work for direct-to-consumer companies, TV commercials can be insanely overpriced if they're used for just brand awareness with "vanilla" creative—such as a car driving down a hill with a generic statement on the screen.

When it comes to amplification, a common mistake brands and businesses make is overpaying for major celebrity endorsements. Many businesses have a dream A-list partner in mind. They think, "If I can just get that person to post about my product, I'll be set." The reality is, that post may not drive as much sales as people think. Instead of relying on one person or one endorsement, consider a broader influencer marketing strategy. You could send product samples to a list of micro-influencers—people whose opinions hold a large weight among their own little network, even if it's 1,000 followers. You could also send products to emerging creators in your field on TikTok—with the interest graph algorithm, their video about your product might drive more sales than an endorsement from the biggest celebrity in your space.

If you have a small restaurant or a store, you could also invite local influencers to your business for meet-and-greets, or host fun events such as a trivia night or game night. Influencers can often be the catalysts who can draw people in your community to your business location. From there you can film the event itself, and distribute clips from that footage across platforms to get even more distribution.

Remember, the influencers you bring out to your location don't necessarily have to have hundreds of thousands or millions of followers. In fact, several small micro-influencers in your area who you find through TikTok or Instagram search may be able promote the experience and create excitement with a substantial portion of your local area. The most important part with these events is to make sure that you film them, so that you maximize the value of content as you post them across advertising platforms

and create excitement for upcoming events.

As you grow into a better practitioner of media buying and amplification, you'll see there are hundreds of variables that factor into this across platforms. Here are a few frameworks and principles to keep in mind:

I. Make sure you have enough creative variations for your ads.

Imagine you're a lawn care service provider who primarily sells to individuals in your town and a few nearby towns as your main customer base. You've been running five total Facebook ads, one contextual to each of the towns in your area. You started out getting a lot of leads, but now, after a couple of months, your lead gen's been cut in half and your numbers continue to dwindle. What would you do?

You'd be stunned how many lawn care and landscaping businesses have asked me this exact question in my emails, DMs, or at the airport when I'm traveling. I'm excited to answer it here (by the way, the answer applies to any local business—whether you're a barber or dog sitter or anything else).

The answer to this question is, you need fifty-five more ads. You relied on the five ads too much.

As I've said many times throughout this book, creative is the variable of success. Even though I believe the Super Bowl commercial is the greatest ad buy in advertising at $7 million in 2023, if that thirty-second video is boring and forgettable, you might have wasted all that money. Even though the media itself was a good deal.

Same thing in this example with the lawn care service provider. Facebook works. It works big-time for local businesses. The problem is, the same people have seen your five ads over and over. The people who were going to convert have already converted, and for the rest of them, it's just noise. Ad fatigue has set in (which is what happens when your audience sees your ad so much, they stop paying attention).

So what you need to do is make more content. More videos. More pictures. More text posts. Use different angles, different sayings, different titles, and different hooks. If you talked about lawn health last time, talk about flowers this time. If you talked about spruce trees last time, talk about Japanese maples this time (because if I own a Japanese maple, that ad just might get me, whereas none of the others would). For the record, I don't know what a spruce tree or Japanese maple tree is, but I've hung around my dad, Sasha, enough to have heard those terms.

In many cases, it's small variables that differentiate a winning ad from the ads that don't work. It's the way you say something in the first three seconds of the video. It's the actor or actress who plays in the video. It's a singular word that you change in the title. It's the thumbnail you use in the first frame. If you're only using one style or one message, you're not going to resonate with as many people as you could have.

The bottom line is, you need more content. The work here is not spending money on ads every day. The work is coming up with new creative pieces of content every day that are then supported by the ads. That's how you may get to the outcome you're looking for.

Once again, this goes back to SOC—your content has to be strategic, and you need enough volume of organic content to give yourself the opportunity to have more creative that resonates with your audience.

2. Don't completely dismiss ad platforms because they "don't convert."

Let's say you have a direct-to-consumer company that's been finding success with Facebook ads and YouTube ads, but Tik-Tok ads haven't been getting you nearly as many conversions. You've historically focused more on your paid ads than your organic strategy, and you've been hearing from people in your field that Facebook and YouTube convert better than TikTok for direct response.

In this scenario, a lot of companies would dismiss TikTok, and just stick to Facebook and YouTube instead. But if you're a historian of digital ads, you'd know that people said "Google outperforms Facebook" in the same way during the early to mid 2010s. When there's an emerging platform like a TikTok and there's mass attention on it, the platform is always incentivized to improve direct-response conversion numbers because they want your money.

There are two things I'd do in this situation:

1. Use organic strategy to aggressively build brand, which will drive down your CAC on your performance ads. The more aware people are of your product, the less your CAC will be. In other words, if a toothpaste brand has been putting out content across social and you've been seeing it for a while, and a few weeks later you search "new toothpaste brands" or "i need new toothpaste" in Google, you'll be more likely to click on their sponsored ad in the search results because you've heard of the brand. That's how brand building leads to sales. In the above situation, if you're aggressively executing on your TikTok organic strategy, you may increase conversions from your TikTok ads that way.

2. Putting all your eggs in one basket is never a good idea, especially when consumer attention sits across different advertising platforms. Right now, more direct-to-consumer brands are telling me that they got TikTok working compared to a year ago. That means a year from now, that number will probably double. Don't be like the companies that didn't do Facebook ads in 2011, 2012, 2013, and 2014

because Google and email marketing was converting better than Facebook. Don't be like the brands that told me the yellow pages was "tried and true" and didn't want to run Google Ads in the early 2000s as a result. Those same companies then had to catch up later.

Remember, these platform algorithms will grow and develop over time. Continue to spend 10, 15, or 20 percent of your time on platforms that "don't convert" and try to switch up your content organically to see if something gets you results.

I still occasionally run radio ads for Wine Library because I always want to be trying different mediums—to me, no advertising medium is ever "dead." If there's attention somewhere, it's possible to tell your story there in a way that makes people want to buy.

3. Experiment with different ad objectives, and rely on common sense.

Depending on your objective or your media strategy, you may not always get clear attribution that directly shows that your customers came from watching a video.

Of course, you can take steps to make sure this is set up in the best way possible—you can create unique Twilio or Google Voice numbers that you don't promote anywhere else, so you can tie the value of your marketing efforts to the calls you get to those numbers. Digital ad platforms will also show you how many people converted after watching your ad, or signed up on your lead-gen form.

You can also use other tools like your website analytics (such as Google Analytics); if you had a video dramatically overperform your averages and you noticed an uptick in your organic search traffic on your website on the same day, it's reasonable to assume that the video had some sort of effect.

But there are also many cases where the ROI of building brand on social media isn't as clear. You might have an Instagram Reel that overperforms in views where you're teaching people something related to your area of expertise, where you're not directly pushing a sale. You might amplify the ad without tweaking it much because you're just using it to build brand awareness. In reality, that piece of content might be one that leads people to buy your product or service, but it's not obvious because you can't always directly attribute the sale to that specific piece of content. People might watch your ad and buy three weeks later by going directly to your site because they already know who you are. In this situation, business owners and brands often throw up their hands and say, "My creative didn't work!"

But this is where you need to lean into common sense. The ad is likely going to work because the video already overperformed compared to your average organically. The creative you're running has already been proven—people want to watch it, and therefore it's going to create relevance for your business or brand. As we know, that relevance is what leads to consideration and makes it more likely for them to convert on future ads you run that might have a more direct-response focus.

One thing I always recommend is looking at your overall sales numbers as an indication of whether you're headed in the right direction. You might be getting more sales, consultation calls, or in-store purchases as a result of people going to your website directly three weeks later because they know who you are through your "brand awareness" ads.

After you've really been putting the strategies in this book to practice for sev-

eral months, look at total sales and see if you're headed in the right direction.

4. Optimize your content based on your ad learnings.

Let's say you made a piece of creative that overperformed slightly compared to your organic content average, amplified it through paid ads, and you're still not getting many conversions.

At this point, you can use both your organic and paid data to change some elements up in your content. Maybe from your ad analytics you can see that your three-second views compared to the total impressions your ad got aren't very high. In other words, out of all the people who are being served the ad, not a lot are stopping to watch. In that case, you can dig in even more: Who are the ads being served to? What age groups, demographics, gender? Based on that information, you can tweak the first three seconds of your video to show elements that are more relevant to that group (through your title, the people featured in the video, the words in your captions, or other variables) to catch their attention right away.

Your ad campaign learnings can also help you refine your SOC going forward.

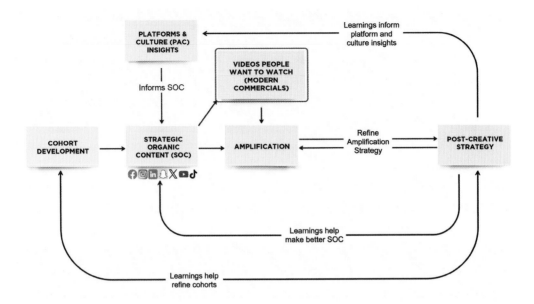

Videos People Want to Watch: Modern Commercials

Depending on your resources, you can create longer-form, broadly relatable, potentially higher-production videos for broader impact. These are videos that might look more like TV commercials that people actually want to watch. The budget for these might be higher than a normal piece of content, but they don't have to cost nearly as much as traditional television commercials do today. In fact, they shouldn't.

Dollar Shave Club's viral video is a classic example. In March 2012, they released a funny video featuring founder Mike Dubin. After releasing this video, they ended up generating 12,000 orders in forty-eight hours. The video cost $4,500 and it was shot in a day.

Purple Mattress had a similar execution with their commercials, leading to $65.5 million in sales in their first year. They have multiple popular commercials. Maybe the most notable one is their four-minute-long "Raw Egg Test," which has 194 million views as of this writing on their YouTube channel.

I believe that videos like these are our generation's version of Nike's "Just Do It," or Wendy's' "Where's the Beef?" They're the ones that capture mass attention, drive culture, and birth major brands.

Especially if you have a direct-to-consumer business or work at a brand, you can create an iconic, higher-production video around your company and distribute it across advertising platforms with the goal of increased distribution. These are videos that evoke emotion like a Super Bowl commercial—they create laughter, sadness, happiness, joy, and they appeal to a broader base of people. Although you could add a call-to-action to these videos to drive an outcome (such as a QR code at the end, a prompt to click the link in your bio, or mention your website link), they shouldn't be blindly focused on promoting your business. These are videos that you'd make in such a way that millions and millions of people would want to watch them. It's like SOC, but more thoughtful, produced, and expanded videos built off your initial marketing insights. The more people who watch it, the more awareness and relevance you'll create around your brand or business, and the more you can drive down your customer acquisition cost as you run ads in the future.

How do you come up with a concept for a broadly relatable video? Let's play out a scenario. Take the following home loans and insurance company, @fox_financial on Instagram, as an example (see the next page).

At the time of this writing, they had 6 videos uploaded on Facebook Reels, and 18 posts uploaded on Instagram Reels. On Instagram, they were getting anywhere between 30 to a little more than 100 views on most videos, and on Facebook, most of their videos got 200–400 views.

There was one clear overperformer on both platforms—a video where they interviewed people on the street and asked them financially related questions. The opening line was "I've got 5 questions, get them all right, win the prize" with text that said "$500" over it, implying that was the prize. On Facebook, it hit 2,200 views for them, and on Instagram it hit 282.

There are a couple of things we might learn from this:

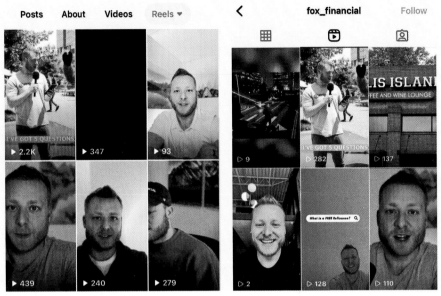

(left) Via Fox Financial–Home Loans & Insurance page on Facebook, (right) @fox_financial on Instagram, both searched on August 23, 2023.

1. It's a signal that people are resonating with the format of "public interviews."

Asking questions related to finance was a clever way of tying their brand into a format that captures attention. If they were to build this concept out into a modern commercial, they could potentially do a two-to-three-minute "game show" style contest with three contestants to see who can answer the most questions right. They might insert a few questions related to home loans and insurance with answers that might be surprising to the broader public.

2. They also had a fox in a mascot suit in the background that represents the company. In the world of advertising, mascots have historically helped companies resonate with more people; in the 1950s, 1960s, and 1970s especially, major brands would incorporate mascots at scale (such as the Marlboro Man, Tony the Tiger, and the Keebler Elves). Even today, mascots like the GEICO gecko, Flo from Progressive, and Jake from State Farm help make the marketing from organizations more palpable.

In this example with Fox Financial, the company could try ten to twenty more pieces of content featuring the mascot more prominently—and maybe try some with the subtitles placed a little higher on the screen so that it's not hidden behind the Facebook Reels user interface.

Maybe the mascot helps answer people's questions about home loans and finance. Similar to how @good-boy.noah on TikTok incorporates a cheetah mascot into his cooking videos as a character who gives advice, the Fox mascot could be a character who helps people out with their home loan and insurance challenges. Maybe the fox interacts with employees in their office. They could continue to build out that mascot's personality over time, and it could become the star of their extended, more "produced," expanded campaigns. Look at what Duolingo is doing with their mascot, which is completely dominating and helping grow the actual business.*

---

* Full disclosure: VaynerMedia works with Duolingo in Latin America.

To remind you, your broadly relatable video doesn't necessarily have to be funny. Humor is an angle that can work depending on your strengths; Mike Dubin had a background in improv theater, so it made sense to lean into that for Dollar Shave Club's video. If you use a mascot, it doesn't have to be a funny one—it can be a thoughtful character, a smart character, or incorporate other characteristics that we really admire in human beings. You could also do a "day in the life" video, around yourself as the founder of your business. If you made a piece of strategic organic content that resonated around your origin story, you could expand on it in a three-minute sentimental sizzle reel talking about how your business got started. I would prefer you make multiple videos—one that's ridiculously funny, one that's inspiring, and others based on the emotion you're trying to appeal to. Instead of subjectively trying to decide which one is best, make them all and post them all organically across platforms to see which one takes off the most.

True Classic Tees ran a variety of high-production videos across platforms with a direct-response focus. Focused on comedy, these videos feature a variety of funny scenarios that their customer base (young men) would relate to. The following video on the next page shows an exchange between a manager and an employee, while other videos feature a group of friends going out to eat or a couple of guys at the gym. This one ends with a CTA to click the link for a 20-percent-off incentive—a brand video with direct-response elements to grow sales.

The themes and concepts of your broad video can be validated through your volume of social media content that you put out, so that by the time you spend the money to do a real production shoot, you know what concepts will resonate.

At this stage, you can also add in various influencers, actors, or actresses who could appeal to a broader base. Local businesses can incorporate what I call "alpha moms"—micro-influencers in local areas who have a small following, but large influence over their small community. You can search your town in Instagram, scroll over and click your town's hashtag, sort by "top posts," tap into various profiles, find people who live in your area who have a follower base, and start to build a relationship. Obviously, you'll have to find the right fit; not everyone would be interested or willing to participate, so you can ask if they'd be willing to

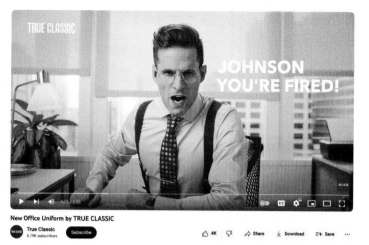

New Office Uniform by TRUE CLASSIC

True Classic
5.79K subscribers   Subscribe   👍 4K   👎   ↪ Share   ⬇ Download   ≡+ Save   ...

come by your store or meet up for dinner. See if they're the kind of person you'd want in your high-production video.

When it comes to Fortune 500 brands, they typically make a few big mistakes when doing high-production shoots like this:

1. They don't distribute the ad in the right places. Running a high-production, emotional ad as a standard thirty-second to one-minute television commercial at the average cost won't give you as much ROI as, say, posting it on YouTube and running it as a pre-roll ad. If it's two or three-plus minutes long, you can make a vertical version of it to post with contextual copy on TikTok, Instagram, Facebook in-feed, LinkedIn, and try the horizontal version on YouTube.

Given the highly produced nature of these videos, you can also run them as ads between shows on OTT platforms (like Hulu), CTV devices like Roku or Amazon Fire TV Stick, and FAST channels like Tubi.

2. They don't maximize the value of their production shoots. If you have the luxury of doing a production shoot with influencers, actors, actresses, or even your own team, you must capture as much content as possible during the shoot. I call this the "sawdust." While you or your team are doing the actual shoot (aka "cutting wood"), you should also be capturing other content to distribute across advertising platforms

(aka "the sawdust"). Maybe while an influencer is getting ready for the shoot you ask them three questions related to your brand's category. Maybe a team member films the production team filming it, which would give you a whole "behind the scenes" series you can publish.

Post-Creative Strategy (PCS): Listening to Actual Consumers and Gathering Insights

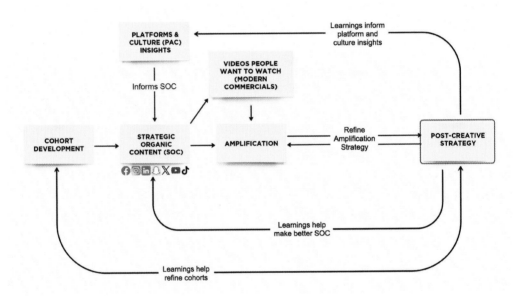

From my first baseball card show at the Jewish Community Center on Oak Tree Road in Edison, New Jersey, to my days working in retail at Wine Library to the present day as chairman of VaynerX, I've done a lot of people watching.

At baseball card shows in my youth, I would walk around the tables for an hour and try to listen to what the buyers and card dealers were talking about. I would try to get a feel for "the current," as I used to call it back then; the overall sentiment of the room. I would watch what made people stop and look at the different tables—I would even pretend I was a regular attendee at the event and walk by my own table just to think about what I could put there that would catch my own personal attention. I listened closely, watched consumer behavior, and used those insights to set up my own table.

At Wine Library, I stood behind the cash register and watched people walk through the store. What direction did they normally walk in? Where did they normally pause and stop? What wines or signs caught their attention? If I placed half bottles of champagne near the register, would people pick them up? I would use these insights to redesign the store layout for higher profitability.

When people look at my career of being an early investor in Facebook, X (Twitter), and Tumblr, and being early on advertising platforms and consumer trends, they often ask me for my "predictions" on what's next. The truth is, I don't predict, I just pay very close attention to what's happening right now, and I act quicker than most. For example, I used to read every post on the forums of the Mark Squires Wine Bulletin Board in 1997, which led to an observation: Wine drinkers were starting to like Australian wines because they're juicy. For the next five years, this category was huge for Wine Library and the wine industry as a whole.

Listening is the foundation for post-creative strategy (PCS). This is the biggest variable that informs my creative process. Once I know what the consumer cares about, I can then ideate and strategize what my marketing and sales strategy should look like. My love for listening is why I fell in love with social media at first; I could post something and get real feedback. Real, unfiltered consumer insights.

Post-creative strategy is about reading the comments on every post you put out to get an insight or an observation on consumer behaviors and interest. Did your content strike a nerve? Are people genuinely leaving positive comments because they like the content, or are they trying to virtue signal to their friends? How do the tone and tenor of your TikTok comments differ from the YouTube comments you receive? Did your content make people uncomfortable? Did they find it funny?

Once you make a piece of content for a cohort and post it, post-creative strategy is about 1) understanding how well (or how poorly) it resonated, and 2) using those insights to inform how you make your next piece of content. You might have made a video for 22–25-year-old females who just got their first job, but based on the comments, you might see that something you said in the video also resonated with older men and women who felt inclined to leave comments with advice to younger people. You might then decide to add 45–50-year-old high-income executives as part of your new set of cohorts and make a piece of content asking them to leave advice to their younger self.

As platforms continue to evolve into an interest-graph-led algorithm, you might notice that your content gets served to groups that you might not have expected. Small variables can shift your content's trajectory of distribution—it could be the way you say a particular word; it could be a facial expression that you make. It could be something entirely unintentional. Like an accordion, your cohort categories will always be shrinking and expanding based on these observations.

You can use these insights to refine what you make for SOC and even uncover new PAC signals. PCS is about saying "Hey, we need to make more videos where we showcase our flowers in the first three seconds of the video because people are noticing them," or "It seems like twenty-two-year-olds value flexible work environments; we need to highlight that part of our company culture."

If you're a business owner or aspiring creator, one of the best things you can do before you make your first Facebook Reel or TikTok is to spend some time scrolling through other people's posts in your industry. Type in "car dealership," "dentist," or "fitness" on TikTok search. Notice the formats they're using. Notice the themes they're talking about. Notice what types of content are doing well, and which ones aren't. Read their comments too. I often get DMs with questions like "I'm running out of content ideas, what should I do?" My response? Spend more time listening. You'll be surprised by how much you can learn about consumers in your industry and what's going through their head by browsing.

When typing in "car dealerships" on TikTok search, one of the suggested search terms was "dealership red flags." See the next page for those search results.

If you have a car dealership, a content series titled "Car dealership red flags" could be an educational content pillar for you that might perform well on TikTok, based on this observation.

Let's go a little deeper:

Clicking into the first video, on the top left, we see a short, seven-second video from a Florida-based car dealer. The video has 645K likes, 4.3K comments, and 22.6K saves from what we can see;

Dealership red flags, searched August 15, 2023.

clearly, it's a piece of content that struck a nerve.

The video starts with a large title, "Car Dealership Red Flags, Part 1." It starts off like an educational skit between a salesperson and a customer but quickly cuts short when the salesperson almost punches the customer (in a funny way) when she asks a question.

Now let's extract some post-creative strategy insights.

Reading through the comments (see the next page), it seems like the overall sentiment was generally positive, with various comments from users that signaled the video was funny.

But what led to the outsized success of this video? Here's one potential reason: Some portion of the public has negative feelings toward dealerships, and these kinds of funny videos can help humanize them. Some people view dealerships as a place for hard negotiations and stressful conversations, and this video presents that environment as a fun, casual place to be. You can see that one of the commenters even names the staff member in the skit, as did the original poster's account when they replied to the second comment.

The fact that "car dealership red flags"

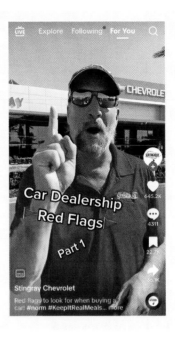

98gabs98
i have a blue trax & didn't get punched by norm. i feel betrayed by my dealership 😅
2021-9-13   Reply   💗   ♡ 3837   🖓

View 12 replies

Teej
So you handin our free fades? Where's the red flag
2021-9-13   Reply   💗   ♡ 6307   🖓

Stingray Chevrolet · Creator
Norm hands out free fades all day long 🐗
2021-9-13   Reply   ♡ 2811   🖓

was already a popular search term means that a lot of people probably feel stressed-out or anxious walking into these dealerships in the first place.

Based on that PCS insight, if you're in this industry maybe you could experiment with funny back-and-forth involving certain customers or staff members who are willing to role-play funny scenarios. You could also work on building up the personal brands of the individuals who work at your dealership, so your audience feels affinity toward them as well as your company.

Post-creative strategy is about coming

up with these kinds of human behavior observations based on the qualitative data.

From a SOC and PAC standpoint, we can analyze this piece of content further:

Since videos automatically repeat from the beginning once you finish watching them on TikTok, it could be that short skits like the one above have a better chance of getting high watch-time rates (and therefore greater distribution on the platform). The first three seconds of this video also had a large, noticeable title that gets people curious—people always want to know what to "look out for" in their day-to-day lives, and this video plays into that. The person in the video says the title out loud, which can help reinforce the title and add to the strength of the hook.

If you're struggling to think of what content to create, you'll find the answers through listening. Platforms like Reddit or Quora are also fruitful grounds to gather PCS insights—you can see what kinds of questions people are asking in different categories, within different topics and subreddits. You could answer those questions in video form on social media.

As you begin to deeply understand your audience and the audience of companies that are slightly "adjacent" to your category, you can start getting into some exciting territory. For example, you can begin to strategically think about collaborations, and cross-promote your communities with other influencers, brands, and businesses. This is something that many personal brands, thought leaders, and creators tend to do well—by going on someone else's podcast in a category close to yours, you can get exposure to their audience and create affinity with some of them.

At VaynerMedia, we have a job title called "post-creative strategist." Their primary job is to read every comment that our clients' posts get and make observations from those comments that inform our overall content strategy. I think of these strategists as "anthropologists" or "psychologists"—regardless of whether they have that formal background in education or not, they need to have the curiosity and empathy to interpret the human reactions from the comments. You can also think of them as contemporary journalists who are doing the research for an article.

This is different from how brands today approach strategy and creative.

Normally, strategy happens in a silo—a strategist might go and do research for a month (for example) on her own looking at research reports, and then hand those findings off to a creative who will then make a high-budget commercial based on that research. When you're day trading attention in the modern world, the PCS role is critical (whether you do it yourself or you hire someone) because it helps you produce both quantity and quality. You define your cohorts, produce a volume of SOC for them based on PAC insights, amplify the winners with media, and learn from the comments so you can do even better marketing going forward.

Once you get in the habit of reading the comments, the next step is to get in and engage. In 2017, I talked about a concept called the $1.80 strategy. The premise behind this was to leave your "two cents" (your opinion or your overall thoughts—not spam or generic comments like "follow me") on ninety posts a day to build awareness through comments. As I'm writing this in 2023, it's still more relevant than ever. Replying to your comments has always been essential as it builds community and a relationship

with your audience. But today, I believe that comments *are* a form of content.

On LinkedIn, replying to the comments on your posts is especially valuable because when you leave a comment, it's more likely that your people will see that post for a second time in their feed as LinkedIn bumps it up again. Each time you leave a comment on your post (or reply to one), the entire post gets resurfaced in your followers' and connections' feeds.

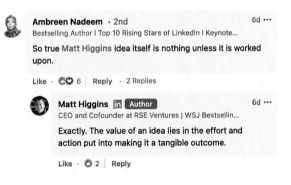

It also helps build depth and relationship with your audience, especially when you can use your reply to build on what they say. For example, notice how Matt Higgins didn't just reply "I agree" to this LinkedIn comment above—he expanded on top of it.

On platforms like TikTok, some of your comments might get more likes than some of your videos. Back to our earlier example with the car dealership a few pages back, they received 2.8K likes on their comment reply alone, which is more than some of the other videos on their TikTok account.

Tone matters, too. Notice how Wendy's built a reputation on snarkiness, as we see here:

When you reply to someone's comment or leave a comment on another account's post, make sure that it's meaningful. Bring value. Be thoughtful, funny, smart, clever, informative; add to the conversation. Leaving generic responses like "cool video" or replying with some fire emojis is nice but won't do as much for you to help you stand out and build awareness.

Comments sections across platforms

have their own capabilities and features that you can take advantage of in your content strategy. Fill in the following chart to audit each platform's comments section capabilities at the time you're reading this.

As we're getting through to the end of part 3, take a step back for a minute and think through which of the core variables come most naturally to you, and which ones seem challenging. Do you feel like

you can intuitively understand the reactions of human beings in the comments, and use that to make your next piece of content? Are you naturally strategic in your thought process? Are you naturally curious about understanding what content works on one platform but not another and why? Are you excited about understanding the psychology of your consumer segmentations?

If you have a B2B company with zero

Comments section worksheet: Fill this out on your own							
	♪	◎	in	👻	X	▶	f
Pin comments							
Post image in comments							
GIF reply							
Post video in comments (and/or reply to comments with video)							
Add clickable link in comments							
Add comments to favorites							
Send comment through DM							

presence on social, maybe your first step right now is to figure out what podcast you're going to start based on the consumer segments you're trying to get as clients. Later you can revisit the SOC and PAC sections of this book as you turn that footage into clips to distribute across platforms.

If you're at a place where you're posting once or twice a week, you could start by getting up to four times a day so you give yourself more opportunities to gather data on what's working and what's not. Then you can revisit the Amplification section to see how you can reach a bigger audience.

If you're a local business that's already been putting out content for a while, maybe you could try out the influencer marketing approach and find the best micro-influencers in your area for in-store events or just broader promotion.

If you're at a Fortune 500 or Fortune 1000 brand that leads with TV commercials as the biggest part of the marketing campaign, maybe you could read through the SOC, PAC, and Amplification sections to see how you can use social to build brand and get marketing insights to help make even better commercials.

If you're already making content and posting regularly, you could pay more attention to the SOC and PAC sections to think through how your content is being optimized for the platform and think through amplification strategies to turn your high-performing organic content into direct-response assets to drive sales.

Don't try to boil the ocean right away. Just start from wherever you're at.

PART 4

PLATFORM OVERVIEW

Think about the different friend circles and groups you're a part of:

You've got your work friends. Your core high school friends. Your family. Your local community tennis club.

As you hang out with each of these different groups of people, chances are you're a slightly different version of yourself. You're still you, but you're in a different mindset based on the context of the group you're in. The environment plays a role too. Think about the dynamic if you were to hang out with your work friends at a bar or five-star restaurant, compared to sitting with them in a boardroom while pitching to a client. It would be very different. Same human beings. Different mindset.

Since social platforms just scale human behavior that already exists, the same concept applies there too.

Humans adapt their behavior to the context of the environment they're in, and each social platform is a different environment with different context, features, and capabilities. That means you need to change how you show up on each platform.

In this sense, different platforms give you the opportunity not only to capture more attention, but also to show slightly different sides of yourself, your business, or your brand. You'll also build a deeper relationship with people who see your content on multiple platforms. It's like this: If you only talk to a friend at work, you wouldn't have as deep of a relationship as you would if you also grabbed drinks with them a few times. If people see your long-form podcast interviews on YouTube and a few twenty-second thoughtful clips on YouTube Shorts and TikTok, they'll have a more complete picture of who you are or what you do. Of course, this also leads to increased relevance, which leads to sales.

If you don't take the time to understand the context of each platform, your content will be less effective at best, and awkward and off-putting at worst.

That's what this section will help you with. As you begin putting the core variables from part 3 into practice, you'll start getting a feel for platform differences. The following pages will give you an overview of what makes each platform unique, and how you can use that uniqueness to your advantage.

TikTok

Many 40–50-year-olds today dress the way they do because they were subconsciously or consciously influenced by hip-hop culture. When I was growing up in the 1980s, the average forty-nine-year-old adult didn't wear baseball caps with jeans and sneakers as their day-to-day outfit, especially not to work. Over the years as hip-hop culture penetrated all different demographics, it has affected everything we do in society—from the clothes we wear to the slang we use in conversations.

If you were around in the 1980s and dismissed the rise of hip-hop as a "fad" or just another "kids' trend," you would have missed out on a rare opportunity to understand a genre that would influence

consumer behavior for the next several decades. Those learnings might have had a life-changing impact on your advertising strategy and your business as a whole.

Just as hip-hop influenced behavior in society at large, TikTok has influenced the way people communicate. TikTok has impacted everything from the size and dimensions of video content to the tone and slang people use when talking to each other. If you've mastered the skill of making content that overperforms on TikTok, you'll likely be able to make content that overperforms on other platforms too (even though each platform still has its own contextual nuances).

Unfortunately, many creators, businesses, and brands across the spectrum dismissed the rise of TikTok in the early days of the platform. Back when I was aggressively putting out content in 2019 and telling people to start posting on TikTok, I heard all kinds of comments:

"This is a fad." "It's for kids and my customer isn't on it." "Will TikTok even last?" "I don't want to lip-sync or dance."

At the time, I had a few responses to these concerns:

1. If you had invested time and resources into making TikTok content and it did disappear for whatever reason, the learnings would translate to other platforms. For example, I spent a lot of time on SocialCam, where users could capture and share videos online and on mobile. It was there that I learned how to create vertical video content; those learnings translated to other platforms like Instagram and Vine, and it was a big reason my content there performed exceptionally well on Instagram from 2017–19. The short-form nature of Vine was what helped me understand some of the dynamics I see working in TikTok content.

2. Even if a platform turns out to be a "fad" and goes away, you'd still retain the brand value that you captured by putting out content there. When you get brand value, people will still find you wherever consumer attention moves next. Diddy still trades on the brand value he got from showing up on MTV. King Bach was successful on Vine first, before building his brand further on other platforms after Vine disappeared. When brands run TV commercials on networks with popular shows, they don't get caught up in questions like "What if the show gets canceled?" They milk the attention while it's there. In fact, platforms like Facebook and X (Twitter) have been around longer than hit TV shows like *Seinfeld* and *M*A*S*H* were.

3. If a platform does stick around, usually it expands its user base to many different demographics. In that case, it would be smart to get on it early and get a sense for how to make content on the platform. The same people who said "TikTok is for kids lip-syncing" would have said "Facebook is just for college kids." Later, they would have had to catch up.

Many of those who jumped on TikTok in 2019 and 2020 experienced incredible growth in both brand and sales. Charli D'Amelio began posting in May 2019 and has amassed 151.1 million followers at the time of writing. It was a combination of her dance talent and the fact that she jumped on the platform early. I even got emails from niche businesses—like cement contractors—who scored big deals with the help of their TikTok content. Can you imagine that?

The platform more than doubled its user base from 2019 to 2021, aging up as it grew. Exact numbers vary, but according to TikTok's CEO, the average TikTok user in the US is an adult well past college age.[15] If you haven't started posting on TikTok yet or you're still doing only one to two posts a week, it's time to ramp up—regardless of whether you're an influencer, a lawyer, or a Fortune 1000 brand.

I've been fascinated by this platform since the early days of Musical.ly, when I invited two stars from the platform on the show in 2016 for *AskGaryVee* Episode 198. Musical.ly intrigued me for a number of reasons; at the time, they were reaching such a young demographic, even kids in first grade. With more kids using devices like iPhones and iPads, I felt that a platform that was able to cap-

ture the attention of the youth would also have the potential to age up to older demographics (similar to how Facebook started with college kids before building a much broader user base).

Musical.ly's early success also had a lot to do with the fact that it provided utility. It wasn't just a social network; it solved a problem. It gave people access to features like video speed control, filters, audio, and other tools that made it easier to make content. Even if you weren't the best at lip syncing, you could still use those tools to express yourself and make content. At the time, I thought the platform had staying power similar to Snapchat, given that they had a similar user base.

That ended up playing out in 2017, when TikTok's parent company, Byte-Dance, acquired Musical.ly, and later merged it with TikTok. Over time, TikTok became the leader of all modern social platforms; at the time of writing, they're the highest-ranked app on Apple's App Store out of all the main platforms in this book. It's largely thanks to the technology behind their For You page, which is built to surface content based on themes you're interested in rather than the people you follow—which is the basis for the modern advertising strategies I'm talking about in this book. To compete in the war for consumer attention, every platform is now trying to copy TikTok's For You page in an attempt to keep users on their platforms for longer (by surfacing content they actually want to consume).

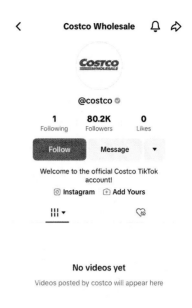

Through their groundbreaking algorithm, TikTok also gave rise to a relatively new phenomenon: interest-based communities. In the past, communities would often gather around personalities and brands, and they still do. However, now because of how content is distributed on TikTok, there are large groups of people who are fans of genres like "#booktok," "#corporatetok," "#sportstok," "#winetok," and more. Two different people may have entirely different For You pages based on their interests—this creates inside jokes and community-specific slang that only exists with certain genres of content. There are both broad trends that spread across TikTok as a whole, as well as interest-specific trends that only people interested in a specific category would be familiar with. Putting out relevant content will help you land in the right For You pages.

For Fortune 500 brands, this presents a huge opportunity for community en-

gagement; some brands may even have established TikTok hashtags around their name with content uploaded from the community that they could engage with. At the time of writing, the hashtag #costco has 12.1 billion views, and #costcotiktok has 2.3 billion views, for example, but their TikTok account has zero posts (see above).

That's a missed opportunity for community building, and it's happening at scale across many large brands.

When users are on TikTok, they're often in a lighthearted mindset, which puts them in the mood for casual, fun content. That doesn't mean you need to dance or be funny; lightheartedness can take many different forms. Maybe it means you type out the title of your video in the app itself, so the font style looks more casual and less "produced." If you're doing an interview series, maybe you could switch up the scene for one of your interviews and film it outside on the park bench instead of in your normal studio, to give it a more casual feel even if you're talking about more serious topics. You could try using more emojis in your copy. You could try using a more casual tone and relatable language through what you're saying. You could use trending templates from CapCut. There are a lot of different ways to do it—experiment for yourself and see what works.

Here are some other factors to consider when you're making TikTok content:

Pay extra attention to the first three seconds of your video.

This matters for every platform, but it matters even more for TikTok—the first three seconds are when a user decides whether your content is relevant to him or her, or not. At the time of writing, it's one of the biggest factors behind how widely your video gets distributed in the For You page, and who it gets distributed to.

This is where you need to call out your cohort segments directly, add titles that hook people to watch your video, state your strong points of view, or add creative camera angle movements that create curiosity. The first three seconds are where you need to show the audience that your video is something they want to watch. One strategy to consider is to make the opening of the video a little more broadly relatable, while the rest of your video remains narrow to what you want to talk about. You might reach some unexpected audiences that way and create relevance with a wider range of people without compromising the "depth" of your content.

The same applies to other content formats that show promise on TikTok at the time of writing—such as carousels, photos, live streaming, and stories. Create curiosity and show that your content is relevant to the people you're trying to reach and do it as fast as humanly possible.

Use TikTok search to find community-specific trends and creative formats.

As I've mentioned a few times in this book, TikTok search can be the ideal place to do consumer research to find popular creative styles for your content. If you have a company that sells office supplies, you can literally type in "office supplies" in TikTok search, and do research. Find out what types of content that group is interested in, what concerns they have, and what they care about.

Search capabilities exist on every platform, but at the time of writing, TikTok and YouTube have the most advanced search features out of all the platforms in this book. You can use search to find common trends and the kinds of language people use within your category. That research could impact how you make content on all platforms.

Interact with the community through comments and video replies.

Comments are a form of content, especially on TikTok.

If you search terms related to your category, watch a bunch of videos, like a few posts, and follow some accounts, you'll get more of those types of posts in your For You page. That'll give you a chance to leave thoughtful comments on posts as they're still getting distribution (which would then lead to more awareness for your comment, and by proxy your own account).

Through video replies, you can build a deeper relationship with the people who comment on your own posts as well, and show viewers that you're listening, which may incentivize even more comments.

Regardless of what your business is, you have to put in the time to get good at making TikTok content. It'll help you make better content for other platforms too.

Instagram

Like TikTok, Instagram is another platform that started out with baked-in utility. Just as Musical.ly and TikTok made people better video editors, Instagram turned people into photographers overnight.

In the early days of the app, photo sharing was a popular function among social platforms. Apps like Path and Tumblr, which were built on this functionality, were also hot back then, as well as Facebook, which had a large percentage of user interactions related to photo sharing at the time. It was one of the reasons why I went on the record in 2011 and said that Facebook was going to buy Instagram.

That following year in April, Facebook did end up buying Instagram for $1 billion; I thought it was a steal, as I mentioned on Piers Morgan's show on CNN the next day after the acquisition, but most of the public thought otherwise. To me it was a no-brainer; Facebook took just a tiny fraction of their market cap at the time to take out a fast-growing competitor and brought them into the fold, and the results have played out. People eventually came around, especially after Facebook offered $3 billion for Snapchat in 2013, and acquired WhatsApp for $19 billion in 2014.

Over time, Instagram continued to add more features beyond just photo sharing. In 2013 they added video-sharing capabilities. In 2016 they added Stories as a feature after the success of Snapchat Stories (and Facebook's failed attempt to buy Snapchat). They also added live streaming, and later added IGTV as a

video feature to build long-form video dynamics similar to YouTube (which was later rebranded to Instagram video). Today Instagram has a wide range of creative units—including Instagram Reels, long-form videos, carousels, images, stories, guides, and more.

Imagine you were a 20–40-year-old living in 1995; on an average day, you'd be reading newspapers, listening to the radio, watching TV, and reading magazines—I think of Instagram as all those mediums wrapped up into one. It's like a "one-stop shop" where people can find all different types of content—they can scroll through images (like a print magazine), they can watch long-form videos (like a full TV show), or they can get value through short-form content (similar to reading a magazine or newspaper article). Instagram is like a "catch-all" for a variety of consumption patterns and content formats—it's like the information and entertainment portal for the world (Facebook has similarities for a slightly older demographic).

Instagram has been making its own push to rival TikTok with interest graph technology—through the Explore page, the Reels tab, and suggested posts in the home feed, they're surfacing more content based on what you're interested in. Given Instagram's maturity as a platform and the changes happening in the algorithm, a lot of creators and businesses have seen their organic reach on the platform steadily decline. It's a natural part of the process. It doesn't mean Instagram doesn't work; **it just means you need to get better at it**.

Here's what you need to consider to win in Instagram's current environment:

Mix up your creative styles.

Instagram has surpassed 2 billion monthly active users—at the time of writing, that's more than the publicly available figures for TikTok, Snapchat, X (Twitter), and LinkedIn. When you're navigating a mature, established platform like Instagram, there's naturally going to be a higher supply of content and ads in people's feeds. When there's a higher supply of content, you need to be much more strategic about everything you make so that it stands out (especially when demand for content remains the same or declines, with Instagram users shifting over to TikTok and other platforms).

When you're getting lower views on your content than you're used to, it's a sign that you need to switch things up. Change up your creative styles, formats, or even the topics you talk about. Instead of only doing Instagram Reels, try more images. If you've been doing images and videos, try more carousels. Try different platform strategies too; for example, when you're posting Reels, maybe try sharing them in the Reels tab only (without sharing them in-feed). Try posting at different times.

At the time of writing, one strategy my team and I have been experimenting with is sharing videos within the second tile of a carousel, with the first tile being a meme or another image. So far, we've been seeing that the carousel version generally reaches more accounts compared to just sharing the video by itself as a reel. We've also been trying graphics that start with "The person who sent you this wants you to know . . ." and finishing with a specific message because we've noticed that getting more "shares" on a post creates dramatic uptick in overall reach. If you would've told me that those posts would be the ones that would reach a million accounts consistently on my page, I wouldn't have believed you. That speaks for the importance of trying different things—you can't always predict the formats that are going to work.

Utilize the range of creative units available.

Instagram has a wide range of creative units, all of which can help you reach different audiences. Carousels, stories, and images can help you reach and engage your existing followers, primarily (at the time of writing). Instagram Reels can help you reach more nonfollowers (at the time of writing). Your broadcast channel can help you reach people directly in their messages. You could also do live streams with guests to reach their audience.

Utilizing all creative units is good advice for any platform you're on, but it will likely result in even more benefits on Instagram because different creative units will help you reach different segments of consumers. If you're only posting Reels and nothing else, you might be missing out on engaging more of your followers. If you're only posting images and carousels, you're probably missing out on potential nonfollower reach. If you're not using stories, you're missing out on sharing a higher volume of content that could give followers a better sense for who you are (such as reshares from X [Twitter] or other more casual content).

Pay extra attention to your Instagram profile hygiene.

Since Instagram is the "catch-all" for content consumption, you can think of your Instagram profile as a modern "home page" for your internet presence. Make sure your Instagram profile is set up properly; have your website linked, have a full bio that describes what you do, and utilize the Highlights feature to showcase different aspects of you or your business. Set up a broadcast channel that people can join where you send valuable, infrequent updates. If you have a phone number that you want people to text, you can set that up in your profile too.

The accounts that you're following can also give people an indication of what all you do. For example, if you have a restaurant in multiple different cities and you have accounts for each one, make sure each account is following the others to create more awareness.

The bottom line is, if you want to win on Instagram, you have to really step up your game. There's a difference between being good at basketball in sixth grade versus college versus the professional league. In a 2024 world, Instagram is now the professional league.

X (Twitter)

X (which I'll refer to as Twitter in this section) holds a special place in my heart because of the impact it had on my early career, and it could hold the same potential for you too. Twitter is how I built my brand from 2007 to 2011, when I was working in Wine Library and nobody knew who I was. I would reply to tweets for hours and hours every day on topics that I had opinions about.

At the time, Twitter was the only platform where you could jump into a stranger's post and leave a reply without coming off as creepy. Of course, now all platforms have that privilege, since that content now revolves around your interests more than your friends.

However, Twitter is still the watercooler of our society. It's the place where people go to share opinions and hot takes about the world today, just like they would at a cocktail party. For brands, businesses, and creators, that means participating in relevant conversations, and using the platform to listen to what consumers care about.

Out of all the platforms in this book, Twitter is the one that has changed the least since I wrote *Jab, Jab, Jab, Right Hook*. Meta is a very different company compared to the early days of Facebook. Amazon transformed into a totally different company since it was founded. The same with Netflix, which started as a DVD rental-by-mail service in 1997. Up until last year (2022), Twitter was still very similar to the platform I signed up for in 2007. Outside of a few changes, such as the addition of Spaces and X Premium (formerly Twitter Blue), the product is largely the same.

When Elon Musk acquired Twitter in 2022 and later renamed it X, everyone was asking me what I thought; I know there's a lot of conversation happening around topics like freedom of speech and who Elon is personally. As a businessman and marketer focused on day trading attention, I'll instead focus my insights where I think I can provide you value. What I'm excited about with the acquisition is how Twitter is going to innovate in the future, and what all they could do given that they essentially own the "town hall" of the internet.

For example, I've always believed that they could launch a streaming service, similar to Hulu or Netflix. When we watch trending shows on Netflix, many of us go to Twitter to share our thoughts; why not build an OTT service directly into the platform?

There has also been some speculation that Musk will bring back Vine; while I have no idea whether that's going to happen or not, I do think that would make a lot of sense. Vine was the platform that popularized short-form video consumption as we know it today, back when it launched in January 2013. In many ways, Vine was the true originator of every platform's strategy nowadays. Integrating Vine back into Twitter or relaunching Vine as a stand-alone app could be a viable play.

Here are some things you should keep in mind on this platform as you integrate it into your strategy:

Use Twitter to listen.

Twitter advanced search is still an incredibly effective tool. Brands can literally type in their brand name, find out what people are saying about them, and jump into conversations. You can search terms related to products or topics in your category to help inform your content strategy across platforms.

This is exactly how I gathered data on what wines people liked, and what consumers were saying about them. I would search topics on summize.com, which Twitter later acquired and used as the underlying technology for Twitter search. I would literally type in "chardonnay" and read through what people were saying. If somebody said something like "I'm going to wine country this weekend to drink some chardonnay," I would reply with a comment like "What kind of chardonnay do you like?" They would reply with a brand. I might hit them back and say, "That brand is overpriced." The convo would keep going back and forth from there. It was an opportunity for one-on-one relationship building. I would literally do this for hours and hours every day to build brand.

It also led to consumer insights. What were people thinking about merlot? I was just one search away from finding out. When I found out that people didn't like merlot at the time and liked pinot noir instead (influenced by the movie *Sideways*), I incorporated those insights into my content. It might have dictated a term I used in a YouTube video, or a theme I decided to cover.

I do the same thing to this day. Because

there's so much conversation happening on Twitter around so many different topics, you can use the search function to get a pulse on what "the world" is thinking and feeling. It could help you learn more about the cohorts you're trying to reach or a cultural trend you might want to tie into your content.

Listening can also open unique opportunities for customer service, and surprise and delight.

Since people turn to Twitter to post about their strong opinions, that also means they're more likely to share their experiences with different products and services. Negativity unfortunately happens to be louder than positivity, so people are more inclined to share negative experiences. At the same time, they're also just one post away from sharing amazing experiences with the world too.

Check out this post, for example, from a Chewy customer:

Searching your brand's name and surprising people with giveaways, answering questions, or being extra kind when someone posts about a frustrating experience can lead to positive word of mouth on this platform.

Post at a high volume.

I always encourage people to post multiple times a day across platforms, but Twitter is one place where you have permission to post at an exceptionally high volume. Even 10–20+ times a day is considered "okay" if you have the capacity to do so.

With a higher volume of tweets, you can try different quotes and messaging styles to see what gets more likes, reposts, replies, and overall impressions. For those of you who are strong writers, posting threads or just writing long posts with X Premium could be a format that suits

Anna Brose, MSc
@alcesanna

I contacted @Chewy last week to see if I could return an unopened bag of my dog's food after he died. They 1) gave me a full refund, 2) told me to donate the food to the shelter, and 3) had flowers delivered today with the gift note signed by the person I talked to??

12:35 AM · Jun 15, 2022

40.6K Reposts   **7,728** Quotes   **695.4K** Likes   **5,758** Bookmarks

your strengths. You can always repurpose your Facebook status updates, LinkedIn text posts, or YouTube Community tab text posts into posts on Twitter.

The bottom line here is, not a lot has

changed, but don't underestimate this platform. There's a huge opportunity for listening to the market as well as getting new eyeballs on your content if you play it right.

LinkedIn

LinkedIn was launched in 2003 as a professional networking platform, used primarily for job searching and recruitment in the early days. What started as a tool for job seekers and recruiters has become one of the most important platforms for marketers.

Today, an enormous number of people go on LinkedIn to get information through articles, news, and other content. The platform continues to remind me of Facebook in 2012, a time when businesses and brands saw high organic reach through Facebook Fan Pages. Though the interest graph algorithm isn't as optimized on LinkedIn (at the time of writing) compared to TikTok, organic reach remains high.

LinkedIn is a gold mine for entrepreneurs, creators, executives, and especially B2B companies and professional

service providers. When people are on the platform, they're in a business and career mindset; it's like the "library" or the "boardroom" of social networks. If you're selling to senior corporate executives or selling a super-niche product that you're struggling to storytell around in places like TikTok and X (Twitter), then LinkedIn may be the place for you.

But it's also a secret weapon for the average business that sells to normal, everyday consumers, such as those selling fitness equipment, wine, clothing, or anything else. Content creators often think of LinkedIn as a cringey, weird, old social network and stay away from it as a result. That's fine, if you want to leave opportunities on the table.

If you're a true practitioner of day trading attention, you know that you need to be wherever people's eyes and ears are, and attention is definitely on LinkedIn. Regardless of whether you're selling to consumers or businesses, you're selling to human beings, and those human beings are on this platform. Make content relevant to a LinkedIn psychology, post consistently, and watch what happens.

Just keep the following points in mind:

Know the difference between company pages and profiles.

LinkedIn users have personal profiles, while companies have their own pages on LinkedIn. Both can create content, but at the time of writing, content from personal profiles tends to get more organic distribution on the platform compared to content from company pages.

It would be smart to have a presence on both; if you're a financial advisor with your own firm, you should be putting out content on both your personal profile and the company page of your firm. In fact, building personal brands around human beings at your company is a strategy I'm passionate about—it would lead to a lot more lead generation for businesses than they realize.

Treat LinkedIn as a content platform, not just a sales engine.

LinkedIn is unique in that it lets users have both "connections" and "followers." Connections are done one-to-one, with people you reach out to (or who reach out to you). Followers are people who can see your content without connecting with you.

A lot of LinkedIn interactions today go something like this:

You get a connection request from someone, you accept, and boom: They immediately message you with a sales pitch for a "consultation call."

Instead of immediately selling to people through private messages and using LinkedIn as an extension of cold emailing or cold calling, consider using the platform as a place to distribute content, and use private messages to build relationships. Don't go in for the sale right away.

Connect with people whom you want to reach, and then make relevant content that they'd want to consume. When you distribute content on LinkedIn, it's more likely that your connections and followers will see your posts. Engage them through your content, create relevance, and then run over performing content as an ad through your company page (tweaked for lead-gen or sales purposes).

As a bonus, when LinkedIn users engage with your posts, your post will also show up in the feeds of *their* connections and followers. If you're selling to people with the title VP of Engineering, you can literally connect with them one-on-one and make content that they'd want to engage with, which would then distribute your post to their network (which likely also includes similar executives you'd want to reach).

When you're making content for LinkedIn, remember to sprinkle in stories about your personal life, your passions, hobbies, and other parts of you that you might not think are "professional." Help people get to know you as a human being as well as your expertise in what you have to offer, and they'll be more likely to do business with you.

Pay extra attention to your copy.

When users are in a business and career mindset, they're more in the mood to read information, just like they read emails or documents at work. This makes your copy on LinkedIn even more important. Regardless of whether you're sharing an image, a video, a PDF, or any other content format, try to add long, thorough copy that provides context.

LinkedIn also offers native articles and newsletters as creative units, which you should absolutely be leveraging.

Use the targeting capabilities of LinkedIn's ad product.

LinkedIn ads tend to be more expensive than ads on other platforms in this book. However, because of their narrow targeting capabilities and the psychology of users when they're on the platform, it has the potential to drive more leads and conversions than other platforms, especially if you're in a specialized industry.

You can target people by job title, seniority, and even the company they work for (among other options). Imagine how nuanced your content can be if you're able to know the names of the individuals whom you're targeting at specific organizations, through LinkedIn search. It's a marketer's gift.

The bottom line for LinkedIn? For influencers and creators, stop thinking you're too cool for it. For businesses and brands, treat it as a content platform, and build up the human beings in your company the best you can. Again, LinkedIn is a gold mine for those who know how to use it.

Facebook

Facebook might be one of the most underestimated and underutilized platforms in this book.

Facebook's the platform all of us are familiar with; it created a monumental culture shift in the early days of social media as the first social platform that most marketers considered to be "legitimate." With roughly 3 billion monthly active users at the time of writing (making it the largest platform in this book), I rarely hear comments from people saying their "customer isn't on Facebook" like I did a decade ago. I'm not kidding; it's the largest platform in this book.

However, most contemporary content creators—especially the ones winning on TikTok and Instagram—are dramatically underestimating the power of Facebook. In their eyes, it's their "mom's social media app." It's the same as businesspeople saying "TikTok is just for kids." It misses the point, and it leads to a lot of untapped opportunities.

Today, a lot of people thirty-plus years old still use the same slang as teenagers or people in their early twenties, as a result of social platforms today. It's what I call the Youthification of Society; if you look at the behavior of a forty-year-old man or woman today, it resembles that of a twenty-five-year-old just a couple of decades ago. Even if Facebook is "your mom and dad's social media app," they're not too far away from being valuable audience members for content creators and influencers that would normally focus on TikTok and Instagram.

Because of the wide range of people on Facebook, and how mature it is as a platform, it's fertile ground for a variety of different businesses, creators, and brands to take advantage of. B2B companies can market to an older audience of executives and stakeholders. If you're a local business, you need to pay extra attention to this platform—when people check Facebook, they're in a mindset of seeing what their high school and college friends are up to. This also puts users in a "hometown," "local" state of mind. They'll be more receptive to businesses that feel "close to home." Not to mention, Facebook will let you run ads to users within a certain mile radius of a location (such as your store). Following the model in this book, you can post organic Facebook Reels, let the algorithm do its thing, and tweak the overperformers to be more sales focused and run them as ads in your area.

I believe that overall, Facebook as a company has been making thoughtful moves when it comes to developing their platform and their brand. In 2021, they introduced Meta, which brings together all their apps and products under one umbrella. I felt that the rebrand to Meta was a game of both offense and defense—it was a defensive move in that Facebook itself was skewing older in its user base and it had been around for a long time, and the name could be associated with an old, outdated product. Fresh branding also helped given all the pressure Facebook was receiving from a political front.

From an offensive standpoint, I believe that the company's greatest strength over the years has been going to where consumer attention actually is. They bought Instagram, they bought WhatsApp, they tried to buy Snapchat, and now they're building the foundation for the metaverse. Meta is playing the same game as I am, and the game I'm hoping you will play: day trading attention.

Keep these points in mind when making Facebook content:

Be sure to mix Facebook Reels into your strategy.

For several years, Facebook went through a period of declined organic reach—like every platform, as they got more mature and the supply of content grew, the attention on each individual piece of content decreased. In the early days of Facebook "Fan Pages" (now just called Facebook Pages), organic reach was high in the first several years, until around 2011–14.

Facebook had to make choices about what content they serve to users first, as most platforms have to do as they grow in maturity and size.

Facebook's EdgeRank algorithm was the first major change in this direction. Until 2009, Facebook's feed showed content chronologically; users would log in and see posts from their friends and pages in the order in which they were posted. The EdgeRank algorithm would analyze your interactions on various posts and use that data to decide what to show you first.

As the algorithm continued to evolve over the years and prioritize relevance, pages started seeing less organic reach, and over time, media publishers and brands stopped giving Facebook the attention it deserves as a platform.

However, as Facebook develops its own interest graph algorithm similar to TikTok and comes up with new creative units, organic reach on the platform is back. Businesses, brands, creators, and influencers have the potential to reach millions of people that don't follow them. Search the platform for Reels related to your business, see what creative formats are working, and start becoming a practitioner.

Use Facebook's analytics to get more strategic.

Like Instagram, Facebook has a wide range of creative units available. From text posts to Reels to GIFs to notes to live streams, there are different ways to engage people on the platform that you need to be experimenting with.

It also offers some of the most comprehensive analytics tools to measure performance, second only to YouTube if we compare it to other platforms in this book at the time of writing. Here are some of the analytics you can see (at the time of writing) on Facebook Reels alone:

➧ Audience retention
➧ Performance by the hour, in terms of engagement and minutes viewed
➧ Followers reached versus nonfollowers reached
➧ How your reel performed compared to the averages on your account, broken down by average three-second views, average minutes viewed, and average reactions, comments, and shares

Facebook also lets you natively A/B test organic content, so you can try, say, two different versions of a text post with two different sentences in your first line and actually see which wording performs best.

The reason I emphasize creative experimentation so much is that many businesses are still running the same old marketing playbook from ten years ago on Facebook. Barbershops continue to post a random picture of their building with "good evening" in the copy or post a random meme with zero connection to the business. Many businesses haven't had practice using the current features of the platform to create more relevant content. **At the end of the day, it is my belief that over 90 percent of the content on social media lacks any level of strategy, even when the goal is to drive business outcomes, which is the biggest reason why I thought it was time to write this book.**

Use Facebook groups to engage communities.

At the time of writing, posting in groups on Facebook is an overlooked opportunity that can help businesses build brand. If you engage in Facebook groups (or even create your own) with the intent of bringing value as opposed to spamming people to buy something, you'd be surprised at the kind of relationships you can build.

It's no different than going to a chamber of commerce to network with people. You don't want to be the guy at the event slinging business cards without listening to the people you're talking to; the same concept applies to Facebook groups.

The bottom line with Facebook is, organic reach is back, and it's time to start paying attention to this platform again.

YouTube

EP 1
Episode 1 – Verite
February 21, 2006

Wine Library's Director of Operations Gary Vaynerchuk launches WINE LIBRARY TV and his vision for it. He then turns his palate toward three commune-specific California Bordeaux-styled blends from the Verite Winery: Joie, Desir, and La Muse.

2001 Verite La Muse Red Meritage

2001 Verite La Joie Red Meritage

2001 Verite Le Desir

Episode 1 of *Wine Library TV* published February 21, 2006, tv.winelibrary.com.

I started *Wine Library TV* back in 2006, about two months after YouTube officially launched to the public.

I thought I was going to do something like QVC (a television network specialized in home shopping). I thought I was going to sell wine on camera for my store, similar to how businesses sell products on QVC.

As we were filming the first episode of that show, I had a lightbulb moment when the camera went on: Once I put this show on YouTube, it was going to be on the internet forever.

At that moment, I realized I didn't just want to sell wine; I wanted people to get value from watching my content—I wanted to build my reputation instead of focusing on the money. This dynamic has played out across platforms today—people who are putting out value with good intent are winning the most. But it's especially true on YouTube, where long-form content can provide extra context on who you are, your intent, and what you have to share.

For me, YouTube was the first time I realized content could drive business. By becoming a "media company" instead of just a wine salesman, more people would become aware of Wine Library, and if they found my content or my personality meaningful, the next time they were searching for wine they might be more inclined to click on a Wine Library Google ad. It's the same principle I'm talking about in this book. By putting out relevant content, you can drive down the customer acquisition cost of your ads.

Today, YouTube remains a great platform for long-form shows. I think of it like a central entertainment hub. When on YouTube, people are in a mindset of wanting to consume television and film-like content with a scattering of TikTok-like posts through the Shorts feed. YouTube requires more production and more effort from users; when people are on YouTube, they expect higher production value.

Consider the following points as you make YouTube content:

Lean into the science behind the art.

Google's DNA had a profound impact on YouTube, since they bought the company for $1.65 billion in 2006. YouTube has benefited from Google's strength in data analytics. At the time of writing, YouTube has the most advanced analytics capabilities of any platform in this book.

The data you can see on YouTube is comprehensive; from click-through rates on your thumbnails to audience retention graphs to seeing the percentage of people who swiped away on your Shorts without viewing them, there's a lot you can dive into. People who are winning the most on YouTube are the ones who are paying close attention to their analytics, and optimizing videos based on that. You need to be committed to understanding the small variables that make a big difference in the results your videos get.

Whether it's large text versus small text, adding someone's face on the thumbnail, the facial expression the person makes, or adding a transparent background versus solid background, it all matters. Testing variations of videos can help on any platform, but it's especially helpful on YouTube because the platform lets you see the impact in views and click-through rates when you change your thumbnail or title. The most successful YouTubers (like Mr. Beast) are doing this at the highest levels.

There are two sides of making great content: science and art. While both matter, YouTube is the place where you'd want to lean a little more into the "science" side of things.

Use YouTube to "document" events.

The cinematic nature of YouTube makes it an ideal place for vlog (video blog) content. There's a reason why people like Casey Neistat have historically done well on this platform, and why I kept YouTube as the primary home for my vlog, *DailyVee*.

It's a place for "day in the life" style videos that document aspects of your life or business, or other higher-production "modern-day commercials." It's especially true in a world with connected TV devices, where people can watch YouTube on television. In fact, some stats show that nearly half of YouTube viewership[16] happens on TV screens—the psychology of what people expect when turning on TV is like the psychology when they're on YouTube.

Similar to TV, another way to document is through live streaming. You'd be stunned how many people would be interested in watching podcast interviews that are one to two hours or longer on YouTube. With YouTube mobile, users can keep the video playing in the background while they're doing other things on their phone, which also lets them listen passively while they're walking the dog or doing the dishes (similar to how they'd listen to actual podcasts on the podcast app).

Live streaming a long-form podcast on YouTube does two things: 1) You're live streaming a show, which is an easy way to make content, and 2) once the live stream ends, you're left with a long-form video on YouTube that you can then retitle with SEO in mind and add a smart thumbnail to it.

Optimize your videos for searchability.

Google's dominance in search carried through to YouTube over the years. Today, YouTube is the world's second-largest search engine—if you title your videos properly with keywords in mind, your videos could show up not only in YouTube search results, but also Google search results.

This is especially valuable for those of you who provide specialized services, or B2B companies that sell specialized products.

For example, if you're a real estate agent selling homes in Newton, Massachusetts, you could make videos talking about the town and post them on You-Tube with the town name in the title. When people are looking to move to the area, they'll type in things like "Schools in Newton, MA," or "Living in Newton, MA" on YouTube, and you can create awareness by popping up in those results.

If you're a B2B company, in addition to posting content on LinkedIn, you can post how-to video content on YouTube; these could be valuable for you even months or years down the line, as people in your target cohorts search those keywords.

The bottom line for YouTube: Once you've gotten off the ground and started posting a lot, use the analytics insights to your advantage, and test everything relentlessly. Be more thoughtful about your production.

Snapchat

User behavior on Snapchat is much closer to how we communicate face-to-face than any other social network.

When you pass by a friend in the hallway and say "What's up?" to him or her, that moment "disappears." For those of us who grew up in the era prior to text messaging, those minutes we spent talking to our friends on the phone every night also "disappeared." Broadcast TV also worked in a similar way, before tools like DVR came along; once the broadcast aired, that was it.

Similarly, Snapchat offered disappearing messages, which played into that dynamic. Its early appeal had to do with two fundamental human behavior truths: 1) Kids don't want to hang out in the same place as their parents, and 2) you'd prefer to lock your room instead of keeping it open.

Like every new technology, the public dismissed it at the beginning, labeling it as an app that had no other use case besides sending inappropriate messages. Over time, Snapchat came out with additional features that made it more than just a messaging platform. In 2013, they released the groundbreaking Stories feature, where users could add their "snaps" and keep them up for twenty-four hours for their followers to see. The functionality of Stories is what separated Snapchat from other platforms in the early days; the feature itself was unique, and on top of that, it gave birth to new user behaviors such as swiping up and to the side, which were relatively new at the time. Snapchat had its big moment in 2015, when DJ Khaled got lost while riding a Jet Ski and shared his hilarious documentation of that experience on the platform. His videos went viral, received widespread press coverage, and introduced a broader audience to the platform and to him.

Just a couple of years or so after Snapchat launched, their early success led to Facebook offering to buy the app for $3 billion, which they declined, choosing to execute on filling the social pipelines that other platforms had ignored.

Today Snapchat remains just a little different from the other platforms in this book. For one, it still hasn't aged up as much as platforms like TikTok or Instagram. Second, it's often used as a messaging platform more than a tool for content discovery. It continues to overindex with the young, and it's a place where people nurture intimate relationships with their core friend group. Snapchat offers two primary methods of content discovery, at the time of writing: 1) a "Spotlight" tab, which is Snapchat's version of the For You page, and 2) Snapchat Discover, which features content from certain publishers and influencers. Most young people typically turn to TikTok, YouTube, or Instagram to find new content before Snapchat, but this platform is still worth keeping in mind.

At the time of writing, Snapchat Spotlight offers wide variations in content performance; in other words, one of your videos could get 17 views, and another could get 100,000. All platforms have these variations to some degree with the TikTokification of social media, but Snapchat's differences can be wider than most, depending on the kinds of content you're putting out. It's a sign that Snapchat is still relatively early in terms of its maturity as a content platform, which means it should be on your radar.

Of course, depending on the type of business you have, Snapchat may or may not be a priority platform for you—a company selling B2B insurance, for example, is more suited to LinkedIn and Facebook than a Snapchat environment, but I would recommend that everyone at least maintain a presence on Snapchat. Take some of the videos you're posting on TikTok and other platforms, make them contextual to Snapchat (say, by overlaying text on the video using in-app features), and keep posting. Be aware of the unique features that the platform offers, such as their augmented reality (AR) lens builder tools, and get practice us-

ing them. In fact, Snapchat is one of the most advanced AR platforms, and as AR still has potential to grow, this is a great place to start practicing your skills as we go into the next generation of innovation.

If you have a local business, Snapchat is a platform you should be looking into. Local-based content is very much a part of Snapchat's DNA, which allows users to share their location with friends on a map within the app. Running ads within a small radius of your business location could potentially help you reach a new audience at a relatively low cost.

The bottom line: If TikTok, LinkedIn, YouTube, Instagram, X (Twitter), and Facebook are all part of your "main dish," keep Snapchat as a side dish, so that you're not caught off guard if or when it ages up.

BREAKING DOWN CONTENT EXAMPLES

Everything we've covered so far in this book—from the core variables of modern advertising to consumer psychology on various platforms—is aimed at one thing: helping you make relevant content.

There's both science and art that goes into making quality content that people want to consume; they both matter. Parts 3 and 4 of this book explored the "science" side, going super deep into the modern advertising framework and platform psychology. In part 5, we'll look at the "art" side of things. In the following pages, you'll see some examples of different content formats and styles that will inspire your own creative process as you start making. I want to give an enormous shout-out to Team GaryVee and many VaynerMedia executives who helped me with this section.

Let's get into it.

Straight-to-Camera Selfie Videos

I'm starting this section with a video from @ucanoutdoors on Instagram because it's a perfect example of what I mean when I say, "Quit overthinking, start doing."

Content doesn't have to be fancy to work—it can be as simple as looking into the front-facing camera on your phone and talking about what you believe in.

In this case, the creator of the video pulled out his phone and shared his thoughts while taking a walk through

the woods. He layered some audio over it from Instagram and added captions for easier consumption. Of course, there are little things here that could be improved; maybe adding a title to the top of the video would improve performance, maybe cutting out the pause at the beginning of the video would improve performance, or maybe longer copy around what the quote means to him would improve performance.

But the main thing I want to call out here is that posting is better than not posting. A lot of creators and businesses can easily execute on this content format. Just pick a common piece of advice you give your customers, clients, or something you believe in, and literally make a piece of content with it right now. You could combine this with an activity you enjoy doing; if you like hiking or walking on the treadmill, pull out your phone when a thought hits you and record some content. It could also be super mundane; while you're reading this right now, you could be on a park bench, and you could grab your phone and make a piece of content. For others, you're reading this on a bus, and even though it's loud and noisy, you can still pull out your phone and make a video. Even if the background noise is a little loud, if your video is deep and real

and authentic to you, it has tremendous potential to be a piece of content or ad that resonates with the audience.

Through straight-to-camera videos, you can connect with audiences in a deeper way, like the video above from food critic Keith Lee.

What he did in this video is what a lot more influencers and creators should do: break the fourth wall with their audience and share personal stories about their journey and genuine moments from their everyday lives.

This kind of authentic, "in the moment" content through straight-to-camera videos helps build a closer connection with

the audience and leads to building an actual engaged community. If you scroll through some of the comments on the original post, you'll see the kind of positive sentiment that it got:

Even if people look to you for your professional advice or opinions, consider sharing content when you hit milestones in life or other personal stories that are meaningful to you. They're easy to make (just record selfie-style on your front-facing camera) and will give people more opportunities to relate to you.

Mascot-Driven Content

Using mascots is something I've mentioned in this book a few times because I really want you to consider experimenting with it. Whether you're a small business or a large brand, there are many creative ways to incorporate mascots into your content—whether it's a full-blown cartoon, or just starting small by using face filters on your product.

Here's an example from the Empire State Building's TikTok account.

By using TikTok's in-app effects, the team behind this account was able to layer on an "eyes and mouth" effect, and

literally humanize a building by making it "talk." Through this filter, the Empire State Building can take part in conversations and have a personality of its own. If you sell a physical product of any sort, you can use in-app effects like these to give your product personality that makes it fun and relevant to the people you're trying to reach—maybe even have your products "interact" with competitors' products or do mini skits of your own.

A 2.0 version of this is what Target did in the following example—integrating a mascot with a cultural trend:

Target does three things right here:

1. Hopping on a timely trend is always a good idea. In the summer of 2023, there were some videos that spread across the internet showing the brand-new Sphere entertainment venue in Las Vegas, Nevada. Quickly there were a lot of memes of individuals and brands putting themselves on the Sphere and riding that trend.

2. They humanized the "red ball" (the

ones typically outside of Target stores) and placed it in the Sphere.

3. They successfully built on an "inside joke" with their customers through the text overlaid on top of the video, "me explaining what happens in target stays in target." The copy builds on it too.

That being said, the best part about participating in a social media trend is the opportunity to keep the conversation going past the life span of that one particular video. At the time of writing, there's some missed opportunity to interact with the comments.

When you respond to comments on your content with video replies within a short time frame, it can help both pieces of content (both the original video and the reply) get even more distribution. For example, when people scroll through the comments of the original video, they'll see your video reply (likely near the top of the comments section, as platforms tend to prioritize comments with replies from the original creator). As people see your video reply in their normal feed as they're scrolling through, they'll be able to click on the comment you replied to and see your original video.

By hitting their comments section

hard with clever responses and video replies, Target could have built on the momentum of this trend even more.

Cartoons and Comics

The ultimate version of creating a mascot is creating a full-blown cartoon character with its own social accounts and its own story line, like Tubby Nugget (see example on the next page).

Tubby Nugget is a cute and adorable character that's easy to fall in love with—the creators publish comic strips with this character as well as actual video animations. It also leads to new business opportunities—at the time of writing, Tubby Nugget's creators sell their own plush toys, personalized videos, pins, stickers, and more. If you build up a mascot around, say, a roofing business, that mascot could not only help your content get more distribution—it could also lead to a whole new "merchandise division" for your company a few years later with people who want to wear T-shirts with your mascot on them because they relate to its personal qualities.

Obviously, building out a whole cartoon series requires talent and resources;

for a small business or brand, it might be more practical to start by layering an in-app face filter over a product like in the Empire State Building example and using that to start building out the character. Later, as the business grows and you have more validation that the mascot works to generate business, you can throw more resources at it.

In the Tubby Nugget video, there are a couple of things worth calling out.

First off, it starts with a simulated "Face-Time call." The FaceTime user interface is something that a lot of people are familiar with—leveraging design elements that are familiar to your audience can help catch attention at the beginning of a video. The audio once the "call" starts also sounds a little like the audio that comes from a phone call, which helps add to it.

It's also built for shareability—in this "call," Tubby Nugget checks on the viewer, asking them if they're doing well and taking care of themselves. People may use Facebook's share feature to send the video to people that they want to check in on, like the person who left the following comment on the video:

One of the questions to ask here would be, does starting with the FaceTime call design perform better, or is the character itself a better hook? If the video started with the character right away, would the video catch more attention because it went straight into the message with-

out making people wait for even half a second?

The copy could also incentivize share-ability even further. Maybe a second line could have been added, like "The person who sent you this wants to make sure you're okay."

Strategic Reposts

You can repost content from one platform to another, if you keep your content contextual and native to the platform.

For example, here's a Facebook post from McDonald's:

And to the right, check out their Instagram post with the same text.

On Instagram, they posted the same message—but since the platform tends to have a more visual feel to it, they embedded the text from the Facebook status update in an X (Twitter) style graphic that's sized appropriately for Instagram.

Also, did you catch the date on the two posts? Their Facebook post was published in September 2022, while their

Instagram post went up in November 2020; this speaks to a concept that I call the "Rolling Stones Rule."

Rock bands like the Rolling Stones could go around the world and play the same few songs repeatedly, and people would still come out and listen for decades. When you have a message that resonates—whether it's an ad, a song, a piece of art, some content, or anything else—you can repost it again and again, and still get traction on it.

In this example, also notice the wording of the message, "One day, you ordered a Happy Meal for the last time and you didn't even know it." The way this is phrased plays into some other similar sayings that have gone around the internet for years.

When searching similar phrases on TikTok, we see more popular videos with text like "When you realize we all went outside to play for the last time not knowing it'd be the last time."

This is what you could consider an "evergreen trend." These kinds of words and phrases touch on something deeper in the human spirit, which is why they've continued to resonate over the course of years.

The way McDonald's phrased their post plays into this trend, which helps

"When you realize that was the last time," searched on TikTok, September 2, 2023.

with distribution, and allows them to repost it from time to time.

Here's another, even simpler example of content repurposing from Deion

"Coach Prime" Sanders. He starts with an X (Twitter) post:

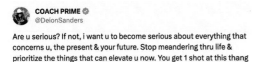

And then trims the elements around it for an Instagram post:

By this point, you've probably seen these "tweet graphics" on various accounts all over social. Like Deion did here, you can repurpose your X (Twitter) posts into graphics. Just screenshot the tweet, clean up some elements around it, and it's ready to be posted across any platform that allows for stand-alone images.

Because X (Twitter) is the "water-cooler" of our society, people are in a mindset to consume hot takes, opinions, or strong points of view when they see a graphic like this pop up in their feeds. It might be the reason it continues to capture attention—creators, brands, and businesses have continued to use this format for years.

Creators have also used X (Twitter) graphics as part of their YouTube thumbnails, and even layered these kinds of posts on top of videos across platforms (so that the tweet appears as the "title" at the top).

Real-Life Backgrounds

Images with real-life backgrounds carry a level of authenticity that's hard to replicate with other formats. Check out these two examples from @selfloveblossom and Chipotle to see what I mean.

By writing a quote on your hand, lay-

chipotle

32,401 likes
chipotle tag ur Chipotle crush 🥺

selfloveblossom

Liked by rosa.lie.la and others
selfloveblossom Reminder! Drop a 🤍 if you agree.
It's not your job to prove that you are loveable!

ering a message on a street sign, writing something on a sidewalk in chalk, or even writing something on a whiteboard and taking a picture of it, you're using graphics that normally catch people's attention in real life. Taking those and putting them on modern advertising platforms can have the same effect. By the way, that was one of the main reasons we used a "caution tape" design style for the cover of this book. It catches attention in real life and therefore might have caught your attention to pick up this book.

You can get these images from stock footage websites and layer on messages on top of them. You could also take pictures of items in your business or industry; if you have a restaurant, use the sidewalk sign outside your building. If you have a B2B company catering to professional audiences, use the whiteboard of a boardroom.

On a similar note, you could also use the user interface designs of apps and devices people use on a day-to-day basis. Remember the earlier Tubby Nugget example where they opened the video with a FaceTime call? There are a thousand different versions of that. For example, if you have an iPhone you know about the

"Reminders" app that sends you notifications with whatever you want to be reminded about. You could add a quote or a message within that same notification style and post it as an image.

You can also create video versions of your brand's messaging layered over real-life signs.

In the above two videos from @theopeninvite, notice how underneath the quote, they've also got their own name displayed. This is important for branding, so people know the quote is associated with your account when the video gets shared.

Now let's go a layer deeper.

At the time of writing, the quote on the blue billboard above has 7.6 million views, while the quote on black background has 106,000. Whenever you get large variability in views on your posts, especially when you're using similar formats, you should analyze why that happened. Variability doesn't need to be large; if you post two quotes on different street signs and one gets 650 views and the other gets 900, you should try to figure out the reason for that difference.

Assuming there was no paid amplification involved in the two videos above, there could be a few reasons for such a wide difference.

Could it be because the white on blue is more readable than the orange on black? Maybe the quote on blue background is just a better quote and should be repurposed across more platforms. Maybe it's worth posting both quotes as text-only posts on Facebook and X (Twitter), to see if the differences there are similar (which might be a good way to compare the performance of quotes by themselves without the variables of other design elements). What if the black background quote was rephrased to "The person who sent you this is so proud of you" on the same exact sign? Would that increase views?

These are the kinds of details you should consider.

Street Interviews

If you've scrolled through TikTok, you've probably seen videos of people interviewing others on the street with a microphone.

It often takes the following form: Two people are usually standing outside, doing a quick interview or just having a conversation. The reason this tends to be an effective content format (at the time of writing) is the same reason why the photos of street signs and billboards tend to do well. Think about the context of the conversation you'd have with someone on the street—it's spontaneous, natural, and real. Its "raw" nature makes it interesting to watch.

You could roll up to people on the street and ask them questions related to your business category, if you feel comfortable doing that, or you could hire someone to do it. You could also do a more structured interview like @themuse on Instagram did (see next page).

This style of content is similar to what Humans of New York leveraged to become such an iconic media company and brand. They posted photos of people with long, in-depth copy about their backstory; in many ways, street interviews are the video form of the same concept. It's a tried-and-true approach.

At the time of writing, this video from @themuse got about 13.4K views, with 373 likes, which isn't necessarily bad, but this is where strategic tweaks could help

boost performance. Most of their street interviews start off in a similar way, with the interviewer asking people, "What do you do for a living?" followed by "What is your salary?" What if they tried flipping the two, starting with the salary first to hook more viewers, and then asking about the person's profession later? Could that increase views and engagement?

Ad Reads

Ad reads are advertisements that are read out loud on audio stations. Historically it's what radio hosts used to do; now podcast hosts do the same.

Like any piece of content, ad reads are best when they "blend in" with the show as much as possible. In other words, they need to be native and contextual to the show. That means the ad should be based on listener interests; you should also consider how the host weaves the ad into the show.

One of the best examples of this happened when I was on *The Pat McAfee Show* in 2017. Todd McComas, one of the guys on Pat's podcast at the time, had a very clever way of weaving in an ad read for Blue Apron into the show, without even pausing for a separate "commercial break." Check it out at garyvee.com/patmcafee2017.

Around the 32:30 mark, I was talking about how I saw the popularity of Grindr as an indication that dating apps would become popular in society at large. Right as there was a pause in conversation, Todd transitioned by saying, "Grindr went mainstream, so did Blue Apron . . ." before going into the rest of the ad read.

It takes skill to execute an ad read like this right in the middle of a conversation. It might not fit the tone of every show, and doing ad reads through standard commercial breaks also works. Still, the more native the content is, the better.

Modern Commercials

Simply put, the best modern commercials are videos that people actually want to watch.

These are advertisements that feel like scenes from a hilarious sitcom, a music video, or an enticing movie trailer. They're not like the standard, vanilla ads we all see on TV with a car driving down a hill and people smiling.

Scan the QR code to the right to learn more about one example that VaynerMedia did for one of our clients, Kimberly-Clark's Scott brand, a company that sells products like toilet paper and paper towels.

We made a horror film trailer called

"The Clogging," featuring a girl who used her prospective in-laws' bathroom and clogged the toilet after using multi-ply toilet paper. The trailer was complete with suspenseful story line and music to build anticipation, capturing the sheer panic we all feel when the toilet water starts rising and overflowing after it's clogged. It felt more like a movie trailer than a traditional ad.

Creating a commercial like this will instantly set you apart in today's world of advertising because so few brands are doing it. Typically, brands only put this level of effort into creating Super Bowl commercials because everyone knows how important ads on the Super Bowl are—but what brands don't realize is, distributing a modern commercial across modern advertising platforms (through, say, YouTube pre-roll ads or ads on streaming services) can also increase the potential for virality as consideration to purchase.

Lenses and Filters

Lenses and filters are interactive content that people can layer on top of their own creations. At the time of writing, multiple platforms in this book let users create

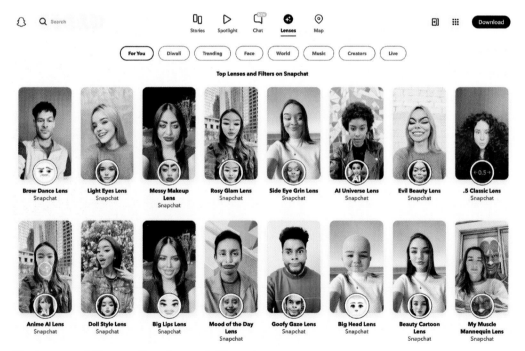

Top lenses and filters on Snapchat, early November 2023.

lenses, including Snapchat, Instagram, and TikTok.

See the prior page for the Snapchat's top lenses and filters at the time of writing.

Notice a pattern?

The best lenses and filters are those that help users express themselves. Back in 2015 and 2016, basically everybody on Snapchat was recording videos of themselves with a bread face or rainbows coming out of their mouth. Today user behavior around filters remains similar, though they're far more versatile than people realize.

Fashion and beauty brands have the most straightforward play here—creating lenses that let people "wear" your product is an interesting move. But there are other ways to play it. You could create an interactive quiz. You could tie this into one of the earlier examples with mascots, for instance, and let people "put on" your mascot's face and share it.

Listicles

Listicles are typically articles written in "list" format; traditionally, people have applied listicles to status updates, articles, or newsletters, but the same concept can be applied to videos as well. Giving people an easy numbered list to follow is a classic, tried-and-true way of making content easier to consume.

Check out how Ryanair put out a Facebook Reel with the title "My top 5 icks about Ryanair" on the next page.

Let's break this down:

First thing we see right off the bat is an engaging hook with a fun transition from a miniature toy plane to a real plane taking off. These types of transitions stand out in a piece of content because they're higher effort, and not everyone can replicate them. They also had text-to-speech read all the text on the video out loud to make it easier to follow along (a feature you can use to add narration to videos without talking over it yourself).

Next, take a step back and think about the concept of the video overall. The premise of a Ryanair video poking fun at their own brand? Brilliant. I really think self-deprecating humor—when done right—is a huge opportunity for a lot of brands out there. By calling out their own flaws or "icks," Ryanair is telling viewers that they don't take themselves

too seriously and that they're aware of how people feel about them. At the same time, the video ends with calling out something that consumers may consider to be an advantage: their price.

Some of you might be thinking, how could it be a good thing to call out the cons of your own company? I'll tell you how—"Perfect" is overrated; people want real. Self-deprecating content helps to humanize this brand and makes them stand out from competitors, since it's such a rare take to see from big advertisers. What may look like a bad play to those who are romantic about traditional

marketing actually becomes a smart and strategic tactic that's helping Ryanair win on relatability. If you sprinkle in some self-deprecating content here and there, it can also make the rest of your advertising resonate even better when you're promoting yourself and asking for sales.

Format-wise, the listicle style of "top 5 icks" is a good way to keep people engaged and watching to cover the five points. This is combined with good visuals throughout the clip with captions and numbers on-screen, making it easy for viewers to follow along with the list.

One of the ways Ryanair could improve further is by reexamining the text on their Facebook Reels thumbnails. Across many of the thumbnails, they have Ryanair branding added to the middle (see below).

Even though it seems small, featuring their brand front and center on their thumbnails might be hurting them by limiting overall reach and views. Here are some other ways to approach it: What if they added the video title on the thumbnail also? What if they switched up the thumbnail text to be more relatable for their cohorts rather than brand-centric? As always, it's worth experimenting with. Maybe the branding could pop up a couple of seconds into the video instead of in the thumbnail (which could help the video get wider reach without compromising on brand value). Another thought: Is the title, "My top 5 icks about Ryanair," actually hurting their reach by featuring the brand name in the title? Could the title be more broadly relatable to reach more people?

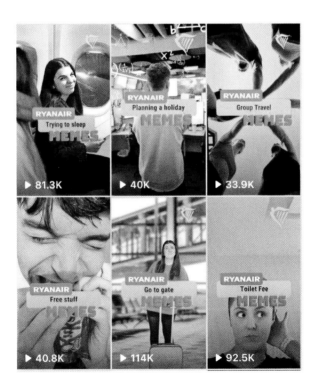

Content with Multiple Actions

I'm a big fan of content where people are doing two things at once. For example, Kevin Hart does a series called *Cold as Balls*, where he and a guest both sit in ice tubs and have a conversation. It's the same premise that the incredibly successful You-Tube show *Hot Ones* was built off of; guests would come on the show, and have a con-versation while eating chicken wings that get progressively spicier. I was on the show in 2017, and for the record, I had the clean-est bones in the history of the show at the time. Check it out at garyvee.com/hotones.

Here's a simple example of this for-mat—a creator talking on video while doing her makeup:

In the example above, it's literally just a three-minute video with the creator sharing facts about herself while doing makeup at the same time. I think people are fascinated watching those who do two things at once; it gives multiple reasons for people to consume your piece of content.

If you have a drone company, why not start a podcast where you and your guest are each flying a drone and talking? If you have a restaurant, why not start a show with you and the guest eating your best menu item while having a conversation?

I've been dying for someone to do a podcast with a double sink setup with the host and guest having a conversation while brushing their teeth. Literally as simple as that. Hopefully someone reading this will take the idea and run with it. I would call it "Brushing up on . . ." followed by whatever category your business falls under.

The opportunities here are endless.

Another version of this content format is producing videos with multiple angles. Take this Athletic Greens video, for example:

The video is split into two different screens—both the top and bottom screen basically show the same thing, but from different angles. The bottom shows a side view of a person using their product, while the top screen shows a more "bird's-eye" view.

Just like the podcast concept of doing two things at once, showing multiple different angles in your video is a way of creating two different hooks. More opportunities to create curiosity and fascination.

Surprise and Delight

Surprise and delight is about proactively doing something nice for your customers or your community. For example, maybe you decide to send a loyal customer something extra, on top of his or her normal order. It could take the form of surprise giveaways, meet-and-greets, sending handwritten notes for people's birthdays, or a ton of other things. Besides just being a nice thing to do, these kinds of acts can create word of mouth by being shared through social platforms, resulting in even more engagement and business down the line. This is a concept I explored in detail in my 2011 book, *The Thank You Economy.*

Check out how @elijahsxtreme uses a clever approach on TikTok to surprise and delight a customer:

@elijahsxtreme used the above video to reply to a comment from a customer who ordered a product from their Tik-Tok Shop. They packed the order live on video and threw in some extra order upgrades as well. It was a great way of not only delighting that customer, but also giving a behind-the-scenes look into how orders are packed, and signaling to other customers that the company cares and listens.

Another version of surprise and delight is giveaways, which you can attach to certain actions that could create more awareness for you or your business (such as "tag 3 friends in the comments for a chance to win"). Check out how Scrub-Daddy did it in this example here:

If you're not careful, however, giveaways can sometimes come off as spammy. We've all seen posts with incentives like "Share this for a chance to win $100." Even if those posts get a lot of shares, it likely won't do much for the brand. Like ScrubDaddy did above, think of giveaways that are relevant to your brand.

Giving away special products tends to be better than giving away money, for example, since it's less transactional and more likely to attract an audience that cares about what you're selling.

It's what some of the biggest celebrities and artists do for their fans. In 2014, Taylor Swift famously surprised a fan who invited her to a bridal shower. Taylor vlogged the whole thing as she flew to Ohio and attended the event (which is live on her YouTube channel at the time of writing). The time she spent to do all this was not "ROI positive" for Taylor, based on what her time is worth; however, the amplification of doing things that make no sense on paper is where all the value comes from.

For all the business owners out there, think about what kinds of surprises, giveaways, and nice things you can do for your customers that would actually be meaningful for them. Even if it's not ROI positive in the short term, the amplification across social platforms is where it gets interesting.

The punch line here is to spend more time "scaling the unscalable." That means doing more high-touch activities grounded in good intent, without the expectation that they will be amplified, but knowing that they could be.

Testing Product Concepts

One of the best ways for companies to use the interest graph algorithm of modern social platforms is to use content to test out what products people are most interested in. If I was starting a drop-shipping (or reselling) business today, I would get as many samples as possible of different products from suppliers, make content with all of them, post it across social platforms, and see which videos overperformed and what products people were interested in based on the comments. I would decide what products to sell after I figured out which ones have actual consumer interest.

The next page shows one way to approach that execution, from @unnecessaryinventions.

In the twenty-two-second video on the next page, Matty Benedetto showcases a bunch of different products he invented, back-to-back. As expected, there are comments on the video from people who are sharing which of the products they actually like, and what they might use.

Insights like these could lead to real business decisions on what products to carry, which ones to cut, which ones to invest in, and potentially what new products to create.

artemis ig
ok but the table is actually kind of cool
2022-10-15   ♡ 11.4K   **Reply**

achim
for me is the bed to charge your phone earpods and apple watch
2022-10-15   ♡ 96   **Reply**

Memes

Memes are a language. They are a way of communicating concepts with tone and energy that can be hard to replicate through written words, audio, or even video. A lot of people dismiss and underestimate new ways of communicating. I, on the other hand, prefer to lean into them.

For example, Morning Brew leaned into humor with this LinkedIn meme (see the next page)—yes, memes can also work on LinkedIn!

Though there are ways to optimize this post further (there always are), it's also just part of the game to get fewer reactions and comments on posts from a LinkedIn company page compared to a profile—hence the 671 reactions for just over 126K followers (at the time of writing).

Overall, since this is contextual to the business psychology of the platform's audience, I think it was a smart move. It was also timely, referencing a 2023 current event with lots of companies beginning to ask their remote employees to come back into the office.

You can use memes to relate to common scenarios that your cohort groups might find themselves in. There are plenty of memes you could make geared toward executives and senior professionals who work in sales, technology, or other industries to mix in with your standard "professional" posts on LinkedIn. You could even try posting a meme and leave the first comment on it with a link to a product demo or your website, and compare that traffic to what you'd get if you wrote up a standard promotional post about signing up for a demo.

Pop Culture Crossovers

Memes are great. Hopping on a trending meme at the moment of peak relevancy is even better. That's what Druski did by tying his personal brand into this Rihanna image that was circulating during Super Bowl 2023.

The meme had proven shareability, and adding his own image attached to it helps with recognition for his own brand. The copy is short, simple, and effective—"Was she looking at ME?!"—and Druski is pointing to himself.

As for potential improvements, the dimensions of this image are rectangular, taking up less space in-feed compared to a larger, more vertical image. Could a larger vertical image get more engagement and reach by taking up more space in the feed? Playing with the dimensions and layouts of your creative is a great way for people to test and learn what formats work best across different platforms. Facebook has an A/B test feature where you can test multiple pieces of content against each other, so you can try multiple different dimensions of the exact same post and see which one gets the most engagement and reach.

Here's another version from @maxgoodrich on Instagram:

He inserted himself into a video with Drake, adding in production effects to make it seem like Drake was interacting with him in the video. Besides the fact that Max smartly weaved his personal brand into this video with a cultural icon, I believe this video worked well because it's a challenging format to execute. This is one that requires some real work and thought behind the production; it's not like other videos where you can just slap on a title and captions and call it a day.

If you're feeling comfortable in your one or two standard creative styles that you're constantly repeating, this is your reminder to challenge yourself and mix it up. Try green screens, cartoons with stick figures, Claymation videos, reenacting skits with toys—you're got to stop falling in love with the way that you always do things.

User-Generated Content (UGC)

User-generated content (UGC) refers to content created by customers or advocates of your business. It's a way of scaling word-of-mouth advertising—if a normal human being recommends something to you, you'll trust that over a corporation recommending something to you. It's just how it works.

How do you maximize UGC? Let's break down this example from Russ:

It all started when someone replied to his TikTok video featuring his song "Handsomer" with the following comment:

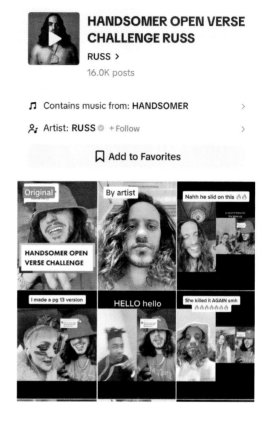

Russ responded with the above video, and people dueted his "open verse challenge" with their own verse while the beat was playing. Russ built on the momentum by dueting those duets, and ultimately choosing a winner to feature on the remix of his song.

What can brands learn from this? You can incentivize users to create content around your business in different ways; you could tie it in with challenges or giveaways. You could say something like "Make a video with the following hashtag for a chance to win a box of eight products from our store." If you own a company that sells frying pans, ask customers to make a video with their best recipes using your product. If you're someone who monetizes your professional expertise, maybe you can ask people to make a video asking you a question, and you can choose the best ones to respond to.

You can use user-generated content to deepen the relationship with a community and create "ambassadors" for your business.

Skits

Skits are great ways to describe real-life scenarios that people experience day-to-day. The reason people love watching skits on social media is the same reason they love watching good Netflix shows or TV shows. Using different characters to play out a relatable scene is a core part of storytelling.

This skit from Tim Davidson on LinkedIn captures common frustrations and challenges people have in the B2B buying process:

The video is a skit where Tim plays two roles, a salesperson and a buyer, and plays out a relatable scenario where the buyer just wants to see the product but the salesperson tries to hold off on showing it to them. Like Tim did in this video, skits are a good way to call out the "elephant in the room" in your industry. In this case, it was about calling out frustrations in the sales process that everyone knows is happening, but no one talks about. It instantly gets people to warm

up to you. There are probably a million scenarios like this that customers and clients have to deal with in your industry. Figure out what those are and consider using skits to storytell around it.

You don't always need a lot of resources or multiple people to produce a skit; just like this example, you can play multiple characters yourself if that feels authentic to you.

If you do have resources or the ability to partner with an influencer who does have the resources, you could do something even more elaborate, like Burberry did in this partnership with @sylvaniandrama:

The video is a skit with a bunch of little characters that @sylvaniandrama typically features in their TikTok videos, but this one creatively weaves in Burberry's Lola Bag into the story line. The skit was so naturally produced that people in the comments section at the time of writing couldn't believe it was a real ad.

That's the perfect reaction for an influencer partnership from a large brand.

Many luxury brands wouldn't allow influencer partnerships with such a casual tone like the above video, which is why this partnership with Burberry and @sylvaniandrama was really cool to see.

Lead-Gen Promotions

A lot of B2B companies use webinar and virtual event registrations as a form of lead generation. In this case, Yext posted a link to a sign-up to a virtual event on their LinkedIn page.

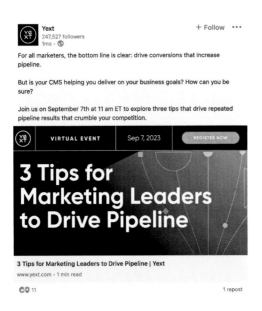

This is a classic "right hook" (aka asking people to sign up) in *Jab, Jab, Jab, Right Hook* terms, which is important to sprinkle in throughout your content.

However, at the time of writing, this post has only 11 reactions despite the fact the company has over 247,000 followers. This isn't a knock on Yext—this is a challenge that a lot of businesses face on LinkedIn and other platforms especially when they post content with a "corporate" feel to it. It's why building up the personal brands of human beings from the organization is potentially so vital; if executives put out content and people begin to trust them, a promotional post from their personal accounts asking people to sign up for a webinar will land very differently than a corporate account asking for the same thing. Building the personal brands of sales team members can also work; potential customers would be more interested in talking to sales reps when they've seen a few dozen valuable posts from them already through LinkedIn or other platforms. If organizations are worried about those team members leaving, they can build up multiple team members so they're not over-reliant on any one human being. Also, once your business establishes itself as a company that's willing to build up the personal brands of employees, you'll notice an explosion of interest in working at your company.

Tactics like these can help grow organic lead gen significantly over time.

Organizations like Yext could also clip videos from past webinars to show people what they're signing up for and share value from prior event speakers. Quotes from past speakers could have been turned into LinkedIn quote graphics, with a link in the comments asking people to sign up for a future webinar.

Green Screen

You can use the green screen format to add your opinion to current events, news, images, or you can green-screen other videos with your reaction. I love this approach because it lets people add commentary on various topics, and it can be a scalable content pillar for many. Search trending topics, find a relevant headline on Google, take a quick screenshot, and record your two cents right from your phone—boom, you have an original piece of content with the potential to provide value and reach new audiences. Green screen is also a native feature on several platforms, so a green screen that you record on Instagram can be posted on multiple platforms with contextual copy.

You've probably seen this format a bunch of times, and I even covered it earlier in this book, so let me show you something a little different:

Through the Gallery Media Group (a VaynerX modern-day media company that includes brands like PureWow and ONE37pm), we've written articles for clients specifically so that influencers and creators can green-screen them for extra distribution.

Here's an example:

ONE37pm started by writing this sponsored article about Lexus vehicles:

Then influencers amplified it by green-screening the article:

This process helps you win in a few ways:

1. You get brand relevance from the article itself.
2. You maximize relevance by getting influencers to advertise your product, and you get their endorsement.
3. By using the green screen format,

chances are the video will get more distribution (at the time of writing).

You can use the green screen format to react to popular videos as they play in the background, review product screenshots in the background, and more. It's a versatile format.

Asking Questions to Gain Insights

People often ask me, "What do I do when I'm running out of ideas for content?"

I always tell them to listen more closely. If I'm ever in a place where I'm confused on what content to make next,

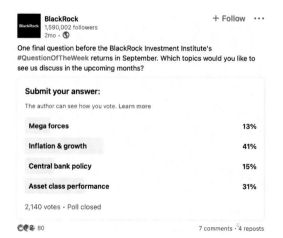

I go straight into listening mode. Asking questions through your content is a great way to gather those insights. Here, investment company BlackRock uses LinkedIn's poll feature to gauge what kinds of topics people would want them to talk about.

Polls can get a lot of engagement, as people who wouldn't normally "like" or comment on a post may still interact with a poll (at the time of writing, the previous poll has 2,140 votes, but just 80 likes and 7 comments).

The broader engagement you get from a poll can give you a better indication for what people are thinking and feeling and inform your future content.

When you're conducting a poll, make sure that you're asking meaningful questions that can help you gain insights. A lot of people ask generic questions in their polls just so they can milk the views and engagement, but if the insights you get aren't helpful, then more views aren't necessarily helpful for your business.

From a strategic perspective, one thing I might have tweaked in the BlackRock poll example is the opening line—when the opening line of your copy or the opening few seconds of your video references terminology that's related to your brand, you immediately lose a lot of people. In this case, they reference "the Black-Rock Investment Institute's #QuestionOf TheWeek." The opening line has to be understandable to the people you're trying to reach—in this case, if they're trying to only reach people who are familiar with their brand or their investment institute, then that's fine, but it likely limited the number of people who paid attention to the poll.

Instead of adding that in the opening line, they could add that as the first comment of the post once it's published, so the brand initiative still gets visibility while also keeping the poll broad. When it comes to the #QuestionOfTheWeek

hashtag they added, it may not be necessary unless 1) it's a popular hashtag and they're trying to get more distribution, or 2) they're trying to source content through the hashtag. For example, in the past I've used branded hashtags like #TeaWithGaryVee or #AskGaryVee when asking people to post questions on social for me to answer. These are terms related to shows around the Gary-Vee brand. But a generic hashtag like #QuestionOfTheWeek can usually be removed from the content without any ramifications, and potentially increase likes, comments, shares, and poll votes (as fewer people click on the hashtag unnecessarily and navigate away from the post). However, you should absolutely try it both ways because hashtags impact ebbs and flows within every platform.

There's another, more creative way of doing polls in video form on the next page.

Creating a looping video with text that says "Pick a Life: A or B" is another way to get insights on what people value. As a bonus, you might also get higher-than-average watch time on your video (since people maybe watch the video multiple times as they're pondering).

The next time you're not sure what to

make, use any one of these formats to ask questions; you might be surprised by what you learn.

In-Person Event Promo

Social media is the gateway to real-life interactions. What I mean by that is, you can take the community that you build on social platforms and deepen that relationship even further through in-person events or meet-and-greets.

Vroman's Bookstore in Pasadena, California, has the right idea in conducting events to create more relevance with the local community. In these two posts, they promote events with authors involving live book readings, interactive sessions with the crowd, and discussions around the book.

Before getting into potential optimizations, let's take a step back and examine

the overall concept. I believe experiential events like this are a great way to build deeper relationships with individuals and turn them into a community, in addition to gaining new customers.

To get the most value out of this, I always recommend filming the in-person events, and distributing that footage in the form of clips across social platforms. If a children's book author is reading their book out loud to a group of parents and kids, for example, or interacting with them through Q&A, sharing those clips

across social could drive more awareness around these events, which could lead to higher turnout. That might lead to even more famous authors hitting up the bookstore to do live events there, which would lead to even greater turnout.

This is where a lot of small business owners and entrepreneurs say "no" too soon—a lot of them say things like "Well, I'm not sure if they'll let us film the event," or "People would be weirded out by that." I respect that, if that's really the case. To this day there are many meetings that I don't film for my own personal content because I sense the other person wouldn't want that or it just feels inappropriate in the moment.

But think about what else you can do that is appropriate. Maybe you can have someone standing by the door as attendees walk in, and ask them if they'd like to answer a quick question on camera. In this example, it might be something like "What was your favorite book to read growing up?" Or if parents are the target cohort, maybe it's a hot-button topic like "Do you think kids should read more?" Maybe you could get ten minutes with the author before or after the event and do an interview with them.

People also tend to worry about whether putting the event on social media would make it less likely for people to show up to the event because they can just "watch it online." I believe for every 1 percent of people who decide to stay at home next time and just watch it online, 10 percent might look at that and decide they want to show up in person the next time. It's a net gain for your business.

Now, back to Vroman's posts.

Both images from the prior posts feature the author directly in the headline, and in the first sentence of the copy, which might have contributed to the relatively low engagement. For those who may not have heard of the author, they might be more excited to come to the event if the headlines were something like "2023 Summer Reading Program for Kids, featuring [author name]." They may not feel affinity toward the author, but they might care about bringing their kids out to a reading program.

This is also where past event footage can help—maybe they could make a Facebook Reel with some snippets of parents walking into the room while kids are reading books and listening to the speaker, and type out the following title on the video directly in the app: "Did you know? There's a summer reading program for kids in Pasadena." In the copy or in the first comment, the bookstore could expand on the details of the specific event they're promoting. It keeps it relevant to a cohort, while also making it a little more interesting.

Notes App Posts

Here's another easy content format for people who don't have time: You can literally type out your thoughts on the notes app on your phone, screenshot it, and post it as a piece of content.

Notes app screenshots have an authentic feel to them. For most people, their notes app contains personal notes, so sharing something from your notes app can feel like you're sharing something straight from the heart. The post to the right is an example from @charlie on Instagram.

The post showcases a few bullets of projects that Charlie is working on, using the notes app to document his journey. Even if this post didn't get high reach, it's potentially good for engagement, helping current followers feel even closer to him and giving them an inside look into his mind, his personality, and his business.

Notes app posts can also be repurposed across multiple platforms. You could share the screenshot on multiple platforms, or you could take that text and post it as a thread on X (Twitter), LinkedIn, YouTube's Community tab, and/or Facebook depending on what feels appropriate.

charlie ⊘   •••

What's next 🚀

- Sept 15th Orlando Fl: The Once Upon A Dream Charity Conference
- September 15th - October 15th: The Small Town Big Dreams Tour across America presented by Kasasa. Making dreams come true all over the country in small towns.
- November 3rd: Best Day Ever. A nationwide event where movement goes out and does 100,000 random acts of kindness all over the country
- Goal to raise $500,000 more dollars for dreamers in need by the end of this year
- Dream 100 mission trip (announcing soon)
- Take once upon a coconut nationwide in every retail chain
- Speakers series at the Dream Factory LA (details coming soon)
- VC fund to help dreamers build their businesses
- Closing the deal for our TV show

Liked by **thornhillwanda** and **others**
charlie Working on some things that will change some peoples lives 🚀

Text over Visual Background

All the music artists reading can learn a lot from Fresco Trey's execution on this video.

If you're an artist, think about all the songs, lines, and concepts that pass through your head. For many of you, 90

percent of it never sees the light of day. If you have a line you're in love with and you're not sure what to do with it, put it out as a little ten-second or twenty-second audio and see how people react to it. Based on the views and engagement it gets on social platforms, you can then decide whether it's worth building out into a full song or even use some of the insights in the comments to inform your creative process.

This example from Fresco Trey is a format that can be replicated by many—play a few lines in the background over a beat, and layer it over a nice, scenic visual. You can do it to promote music that's already out or use it to try new concepts and gauge reactions.

It's not just artists either. Adding text over a scenic background with audio is a format that can work for any business or brand. It's one to consider for people who would prefer to not be on camera.

Using this format, it could be as simple as layering a message you believe over a background that is relevant (such as your office) and adding music or your own voice reading the message out loud.

Visualizing Information

When you're communicating a message, one of the questions to ask yourself is, "How can I make it as easy as possible for someone to understand this?" Visualizing information through graphs, sketches, or charts is one of the ways to achieve this.

For example, Alex Lieberman complements his narration in this video with diagrams that visualize the advice he's giving. The video starts off with a title being written out, and then goes into the drawing.

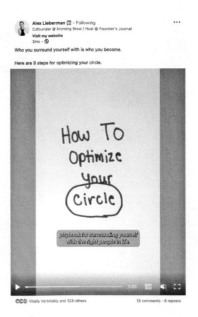

This is a creative style you can consider if you're making "step by step" content. If you're talking about, say, ten steps to optimize your diet, an infographic or a sketch might be easier to follow rather than just saying all ten steps straight to camera in a selfie-style video. A video like this one could also be repurposed into text posts across platforms as well as blog posts and native articles.

Using Products Incorrectly

For anyone who sells a physical product, one genre of content to consider is using your product in unique, potentially incorrect ways. A quick search on TikTok for "using things incorrectly" pulls up some videos that hit millions and millions of views (likely because this kind of content creates surprise and intrigue).

Whether you're using your product incorrectly in a funny way or showcasing a different actual use case that people may not have considered, try playing with this content format and see what you come up with. Maybe it's using exercise equipment as a clothes hanger (which is what often happens in many households) or turning an old shoe into a plant vase. How creative can you get?

Another version of this is mispronouncing your company or product

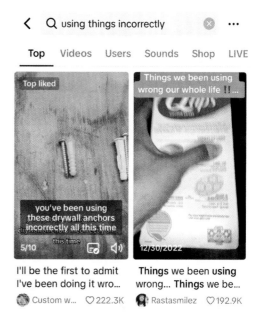

"Using things incorrectly" search on TikTok, October 10, 2023.

name on purpose. Check out this video from Cartier, showing how different people pronounce "Pasha de Cartier":

Content like this is funny and creative and can be a little self-deprecating, which is a good tone to have every now and then.

"Did You Know" Posts

This example is for everyone who thinks they're in an "unsexy" industry that's difficult to storytell around. On the next page is an example of a company that builds sidewalks, driveways, and roads and made a TikTok video over five minutes long that still hit millions of views on their account (at the time of writing).

Here's what you can learn from this:

1. Creating posts with a "Did you know" format makes people curious about what you have to say. In this case, Stellar Sidewalks started their video with the title "I wish more DIYers knew . . ." They called out their target cohort in the title and used a satisfying-to-watch visual in the first few seconds to grab attention.

2. The copy builds on the curiosity the title creates. Here's the core text: "DIYers are always trying to save money, understandably . . . that's the reason they're doing it themselves. When it comes to concrete, there is a huge misconception that mixing your own concrete is cheaper than having a ready mixed concrete company deliver it. Let's take a look at the numbers." It clearly defines a point of view and serves as another "hook" to get people to watch.

3. They added some small details to make the video native to TikTok, such as adding popular audio to the video (at the time of writing).

4. The video is incredibly thorough. They use various online calculators themselves and do calculations in the video, breaking down costs and numbers that bring value to viewers.

Think of the biggest misconceptions people have about your industry. What are the mistakes your customers make trying to solve their problems on their own? What are they doing that they think is saving them money, but is actually losing them money? What are strong points of view you have? What do you genuinely wish more people knew?

You could talk about all these concepts with a "Did you know" style video.

This kind of content has potential to resonate on all platforms. For example, B2B companies can make "Did you know" videos targeted at chief financial officers at the companies they're trying to sell to, and break down common ways their companies lose money that can be solved with the product. Those videos could be run as ads on LinkedIn directly to those CFOs. This format naturally creates curiosity.

In-App Creator Templates

Some platforms in this book, such as Facebook, Instagram, TikTok, and LinkedIn, provide in-app "templates" for users to create content at the time of writing. Platforms create these features to make it easier for creators to make content; sometimes content made using these in-app templates can get extra distribution, as platforms may want to incentivize more users to use their in-app features.

To the right is a piece of content from Sara Blakely on LinkedIn, made using LinkedIn's in-app "template" feature.

At the time of writing, you can use LinkedIn's mobile app to add text over backgrounds of various colors—an easy way to have your content stand out while remaining contextual to LinkedIn. No excuses that you can't design or edit when the app basically does it for you!

Sara Blakely · Following
Founder of SPANX
5mo ·

When given the opportunity to aim for success or value, always choose value. Success will follow. Wake up each day and focus on how to add value- to your family, neighbors, customers, community, and ultimately the world. The success will follow. And you will be happier!
#Success
#Entrepreneur

The goal is not to be successful. The goal is to be valuable. Once you're valuable, instead of chasing success, it will attract itself to you.

Steph Crededio and 40,525 others   1,165 comments · 5,159 reposts

GIFs

GIFs are animated, "moving" images that loop for a short duration. There's something about this content format that makes them visually appealing and fun to watch over and over again.

At the time of writing, multiple platforms in this book support native GIF uploads—platforms like X (Twitter) and Facebook allow you to upload from Giphy's database. You can add GIFs to your posts to add a layer of fun, and another way to hook people into consuming your content, like Starbucks did here:

In this GIF, Starbucks sketched out someone throwing a paper airplane across the cup, which lands in another stick figure's hands and reads "Starbucks date?" Here are some questions to ask:

Performance-wise, how would a GIF compare to looping video of the same thing? How does that performance differ on, say, Facebook compared to X (Twitter)?

Carousels

Instagram Reels have become the go-to format for a lot of creators, but carousels are a smart play for multiple reasons. Unlike a Reel or a regular in-feed image, a carousel has multiple slides or tiles, which means users have more than one chance to engage with that post on Instagram. You may have noticed that if you scroll past the first tile in a carousel post, Instagram will typically serve you the next tile of that same carousel the next time you open the app (at the time of writing). This means the more tiles, the more chances your content will be seen and the higher your potential for likes, comments, and shares.

Here's an example of a carousel format that I've been doing in my Instagram content:

As I mentioned earlier in this book, this is a strategy that's been working for my content at the time of writing; my team and I have been trying a broadly relatable quote or meme as the first tile, with a related video as the second tile. We're seeing this reach a higher percentage of people compared to just sharing the video by itself as a reel. Ironically, at the time of the final edit of this book, we're already doing fewer carousels and experimenting with different strategies to get more visibility for Reels; that's how fast all of this moves.

TikTok has carousels too. Here's REI, showcasing a fun way of making a product relevant to a narrow cohort.

The first tile serves as a strong "hook" that might have helped this post get served to dog lovers or people who like this specific breed of dog. With this strategic piece of content, this company that sells gear for outdoor activities was able to create overlap between their business and something people are more broadly interested in. If they had defined their cohort as, say, outdoor recreation enthusiasts who bring their dogs with them on their adventures, this piece of content might have been a good way to make REI products mean something more to them than just another piece of gear.

Also, note how this carousel is not too

fancy or overproduced. In fact, it's just a series of screenshots from a website and some native, in-app text—something you can make entirely on your phone. It's very TikTok-esque: simple and built for lighthearted entertainment.

With this particular post, the copy could have been built out even further. This is where they could've created even more relevance. For example, are there any inside jokes that only dog owners would understand, or owners of this specific breed would understand? Maybe they could have referenced relatable situations that dog owners experience when they take their pets out on a hiking trail or another activity.

Here's another carousel example from X (Twitter):

Uber* leverages the trend of showing dads in "travel mode" who plan everything for the family trip; it plays on cultural relevance. For example, searching "Airport dad" in TikTok pulls up a lot of different videos showing dads focused on making sure everything goes well on the vacation.

Uber does a few different spins on this trend, one for each tile in their X (Twitter) carousel. The first is about the airport dad "making sure the plane exists," the second has the airport dad "checking passports," and the third tile does a spin-off on the travel dad character with the "friend that plans everything." Because these tiles were inspired by trends that were already spreading across TikTok and other platforms, it's more likely

*Full disclosure: I'm an investor.

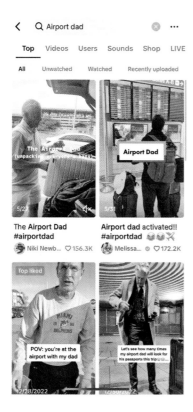

"Airport dad" searched on TikTok, September 4, 2023.

play carousels on LinkedIn at the time of writing is through document uploads (or PDFs). By compiling a PDF with your "tiles," you can upload it as a document on LinkedIn and it will show up somewhat similar to carousels on other platforms.

Our last carousel example on the next page is from Upworthy, a "roundup" post in a carousel format.

For those of you who have multiple different pieces of content going up across platforms, or a week when you have a lot of different business announcements, a carousel post can be a good way to group everything in one place.

In this carousel, Upworthy groups together the "10 moments that made us smile this week," with a promotional message on the last tile to sign up to their email newsletter.

The one thing I would have changed here is the first tile. Whenever you have a carousel where the first tile is a "title" slide (like "5 things you need to know," or in this case, "10 moments that made us smile this week"), it can help to have a CTA on tile 1 asking people to swipe to the other tiles. Especially on Instagram, a percentage of people may not swipe past the first tile when they see the carousel in

that people would want to watch them. You can also use trends on one platform (such as TikTok) to inform your content on another platform, as long as elements like sizing and copy remain contextual.

On LinkedIn, carousels look a little different than other platforms. Since LinkedIn removed their native carousel feature in June 2023, the only way to dis-

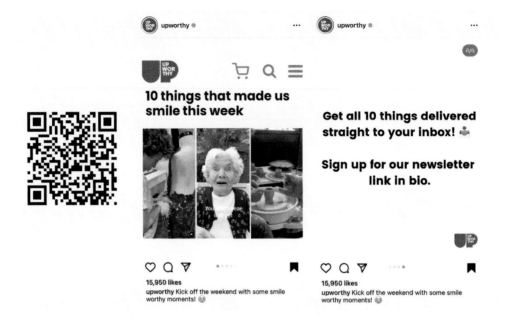

their feed, so it helps to have some text like "swipe to see more" or an animation indicating that there's more content to see.

Text Posts

At the time of writing, Facebook, YouTube, LinkedIn, and X (Twitter) let users publish text posts. By text posts, I'm talking about posts like Facebook's status update feature, where you can write out your thoughts in long form and publish. TikTok also has a version of this at the time of writing, where you can type out text on a blank background and post it as a video.

There are different ways to execute text posts—you could write long copy, a short quote, or even attach an image to it.

Here's one from Ryan Roslansky, currently the CEO of LinkedIn.

This post on LinkedIn by Ryan show-

Ryan Roslansky 🔗 · 1st
CEO at LinkedIn
1yr · 🌐

We live in a world where business cycles are quicker and more nuanced than ever. This creates new opportunities, but requires an adaptive leadership approach. The best leaders are those who get really good at managing through the cycles in their markets and their business. They are the Responsive Leaders - those who ride the waves versus Reactive leaders – those who are thrashed by them.

Responsive Leaders vs. Reactive Leaders:

1. Responsive leaders constantly adapt their playbooks to capitalize on whatever circumstances arise; Reactive leaders write new playbooks to deal with circumstances happening to them.

2. Responsive leaders see cycles as an opportunity; reactive leaders see cycles as a tax and burden to be manage.

3. Responsive leaders realize that these cycles don't hit every part of their business in the same way and have the sophistication to manage nuance; Reactive leaders use blunt tools.

4. Responsive leaders always play to win, though the plays may be different; Reactive leaders cycles between aggressively playing to win and hunkering down.

5. Responsive leaders pivot, iterate and adjust; Reactive leaders over rotate and thrash.

#leadership, Melissa Selcher

Krista Wierzbicki Todd and 2,506 others   130 comments · 89 reposts

and experiences in their industry without overly promoting themselves. Companies frequently treat LinkedIn as a place to PR themselves, but if you act more like a "media company" rather than a "salesperson," you'll be surprised how much more you can sell.

The theme of Ryan's post (leadership) is relevant to the psychology of the audience of LinkedIn who are already in that business mindset. The key points of the post are broken down in listicle format, which makes it easy to read and follow. The hashtag #leadership at the end is a nice touch that may help with distribution. Since users can follow hashtags on LinkedIn (at the time of writing) and occasionally see posts with that hashtag in their feed, there's a chance people who follow the hashtag "leadership" will see Ryan's post too.

cases what a lot of CEOs/executives/companies should be doing on the platform—sharing their observations

Throwback Content

People love nostalgic posts, whether it's a photo of you when you were younger, a picture from the early days of your business, or any other part of your "origin story." Sharing old photos with copy that explains what you were doing in the picture can add another layer of depth to your personality and give people more opportunities to relate to you. If you post a picture of the first dollar you earned at your nail salon with copy of what that meant to you, people might find that inspiring. If you're an accountant and you post a picture of yourself from high school hanging out at the park with your friends, that might humanize you and get more people to consider working with you. These posts may or may not have wide reach, but they're good for creating depth and showing people who you are.

Here's one from Tim Ferriss, on You-Tube.

Just an old photo and text associated with it. Simple.

Another way to build on Tim's post to the right might be to add something like "Throwback Thursday" or "Flashback Friday" to the beginning of the post to make it more relevant for the day of the week.

For those of you with B2B companies or more "professional" industries, this is something you should consider as a

Tim Ferriss
3 days ago

Blast from the past — Me and Alicia Monti competing in the 2005 Buenos Aires Tango Championships Semi-Finals. This is from a round at Salon la Argentina in downtown (Centro). The floors were like slick bathroom tiles.

pillar for your content. You could post weekly "throwback" photos of yourself with a story from your early days.

Quick Takes and Opinions

If you can provide honest, unfiltered opinions about products or services, you'll build an incredible amount of trust with the people consuming your content.

This isn't always easy. Back in my Wine Library days, I would taste wine on video and literally tell the world if I hated it, even if we carried that wine in the store. I know this is challenging for many—if you're a real estate agent, it's hard to make a video and say what parts of town you personally wouldn't want to live in, especially if you need to sell houses in those areas. However, the closer you can get to sharing your honest opinion, especially when it doesn't benefit you professionally, the more trust you'll build.

The following format is an effective way of sharing quick opinions on different topics:

In this video, @CarsJudge on YouTube uses sound effects and hand gestures to convey whether they feel positively, negatively, or so-so about various cars on the street. This format is a fast way of sharing opinions, and it appeals to people who might not want to sit down and watch a longer, more thoughtful video for a deeper explanation. It's easy to understand—when someone points to a car and shows a thumbs-up sign, it's obvious what he or she means. It's similar to my show *Overrated/Underrated*, where I share quick hot takes on a variety of topics in pop culture.

@CarsJudge has multiple Shorts like the above video on their YouTube channel; one of the things I'd recommend trying in the future for more relevance and reach is changing up the titles (both the YouTube Shorts title and the text overlay title that's placed on the video itself).

Multiple videos on the page have the text "Car Mechanic Advice" on the screen, which can make the videos seem like the same one in the minds of viewers. Even if you have a content format that consistently works, it's important to change up certain elements so it still feels fresh. Maybe a different title could be "Car buying advice you shouldn't ignore" or even calling out certain car brands in the title.

The same thing applies to the YouTube Shorts title below the videos in these examples. Although YouTube Shorts will automatically distribute your content through their "Shorts feed," a well-titled short is more likely to be surfaced in search results, as well as on the home page of the app.

#youtubemechanic
#mechanic #cars

Try to follow my advice
#mechanic #shorts...

A lot of businesses can use this format as a content pillar. If you have a hair salon, you might have strong opinions on hair products that are good and bad. If you have a bike repair shop, you probably have opinions on the quality of different brands. As you can see in the example above, you don't need a fancy camera or a studio to film your product reviews—you can use your phone as a video camera and do it all directly in the app on most platforms.

The key is to make sure that you tell the truth.

Incentivizing Engagement

Great content that evokes emotion will naturally get people to engage, but it definitely helps to add calls-to-action and other platform-specific elements to get people to react, comment, share, or save your post.

In the following example, Postmates gamified their Instagram Stories posts using the "tap to go forward" feature.

They asked people to "tap" to break the glass in tile 1 of the story, and by tile 3, they revealed a $100 delivery credit code. Using a gamification element was a fun way of getting viewers to pay attention to each story tile instead of quickly tapping through it to get to the next story.

On a similar note, here's a post I did with the headline "the person who sent you this wants you to know," followed by a sharable message that's revealed after pouring milk in a coffee cup.

Getting people to share a piece of

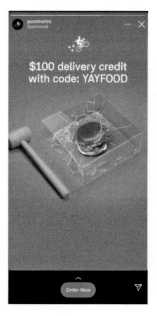

content in their direct messages is a high-value action. In other words, it's often harder to get people to share a piece of content with their friends than it is to "like" a post or even comment on it. If someone shares your post in their messages, it's a signal to the platform that they were really captivated by it, which then increases the likelihood that the post will be shown to more people. Your future posts may also be shown higher up in the feed for those who shared one of your prior posts, since the platform has a sense that you're making content they're interested in.

As you're commenting on posts, you can also incentivize engagement through the copy you write in the comments section. At the time of writing, Instagram lets you "like" comments by tapping a heart to the far right of the comment, and the following user used smart wording in their comment to get thousands and thousands of likes (which also pushed the comment close to the top).

This video has many nice, wholesome comments from people saying nice things about this kid dribbling a basketball. @jxda.peterson on Instagram took it to a different level by 1) describing a senti-

jxda.peterson 13w
get this dude on the court button
———->

16,548 likes   Reply

View all 12 replies

ment people felt, and 2) getting likes from those who felt that way by essentially asking them to tap on the "heart."

The more likes and replies a comment gets, the more likely the platform will push it to the top, which then leads to even more likes and replies. You can drive a significant amount of awareness around your business or brand by just finding creative ways to add your opinion in the comments of other posts. The key is to make sure you're leaving comments on recent posts, or the ones that are relatively early in the process of getting traction, so you give yourself the greatest opportunity for awareness.

Reaction Videos

Reaction videos are a genre of content where people record their spontaneous reactions while watching another piece of content. It's a way of creating relevance through relatability—if you watch another person reacting to a video, it's kind of like you're watching the video for the first time along with them.

Reaction videos were especially popular in the early days of YouTube, but the format is still a solid go-to in the modern social media world. More and more platforms are creating features that make it easier to react to videos. For example, TikTok has a "duet" feature that lets you post your video side by side with another video:

Another version of a "reaction" video is to stitch a video on TikTok; this feature lets you place your video after a short snippet of another video (a five-second snippet, at the time of writing). More and more platforms are replicating these features—currently you can do versions of "duets" and/or "stitches" on Tik-Tok, YouTube, Facebook, and Instagram, though the platforms may call them by different names.

You can use this format to react to popular videos that are related to your industry or what you do; a lawyer analyzing an accident, a chef analyzing a recipe, or a music artist "reacting" to a beat with a song are all different ways of using this format.

Podcast Clips

What Steven Bartlett did here is a classic example of cutting up video clips from long-form podcasts and posting them on social.

In this example, he makes use of Instagram's collaborative post feature to do a collab post with his guest, Barbara Corcoran. Interviewing guests on your podcast gives you the opportunity to turn some of their fans into long-term listeners of your show, and create more awareness around your brand in general.

Since the clip only features Barbara from start to finish, it might have gotten more distribution among Barbara's audience, who might then follow Steven through the collab post feature.

Every podcast host should find their own balance in terms of how much they focus on themselves versus how much they focus on their guests in podcast clips. Featuring more on the guests might help get more distribution among their audience, but you might also want to let your own brand and personality shine through the video.

When it comes to the nuances of this clip, here's one thing you should notice in the graphic on the previous page: the name of the audio. The audio track was labeled "Stop scrolling & watch this" under the username. Whether more people watch the video because of that or not, it shows that Steven is playing with different features that the platform has to offer and trying different ways to catch attention. Trying little things like this is how you eventually uncover small tactics that work.

Authentic Partnerships

The worst thing you can do when working with influencers is let your ego get in the way of how your brand is perceived and try to micromanage their content output. Fortune 500 brands often have ideologies of what their brand "stands for," which I find to be a vulnerability. The reality is that brands mean different things to different people. Influencer marketing, when done right, is an opportunity to let the influencer produce content around his or her interpretation of your brand. You shouldn't try to get them to use terminology that isn't authentic to them—it'll actually hurt your campaign more than it will help because their audience can sniff out their inauthenticity.

This example from MrBeast Burger and Tariq the "corn kid" puts this into practice.

The corn kid has a recognizable and lovable TikTok voice and face. A video where he talked about his love for corn made him famous on the platform, with many TikTok users making their own videos using his audio.

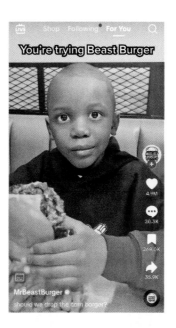

Tariq tries one of MrBeast's burgers and gives his honest two cents—even saying that he likes corn better than the burger. You can tell it's an honest response, which is why it works.

Using the copy, MrBeast Burger asked people "should we drop the corn borger?" It referenced the adorable way in which Tariq pronounced "burger" (his pronunciation of "corn" is part of what touched the hearts of so many and led to the virality of his initial corn video). It also gave MrBeast Burger the opportunity to build on the relevance created from this post, and generate comments on what people think about the new "corn borger" product idea. Whether they actually decided to make it or not depends on their business realities, but the question in copy was a good way to gather insights.

PART 6

REAL-LIFE SCENARIOS

Over the years, I've heard a lot of questions at keynotes, in the airport when I'm traveling, through my messages on social, and through 4Ds (an immersive digital education program through the Sasha Group at VaynerX). Fundamentally, many of the business and marketing questions I get boil down to a handful of similar scenarios.

Based on the exceptionally positive feedback from the "Real-life Scenarios" section from my last book, *Twelve and a Half*, I thought I would do something similar for this book. My team and I created scenarios based on common questions I receive, as well as common situations we see at VaynerX from Fortune 500 brands, influencers, local businesses, B2B companies, direct-to-consumer companies, start-

ups, family businesses, and more. I share my point of view on what I would do if I were in each one of these situations.

As you go through part 6, you'll learn the following:

- How to choose what influencers to work with
- How to make social media content when you have an "unsexy" business
- How to grow your chances of winning a local election
- How to rebrand your product to a luxury item
- What to keep in mind as you're building a social media team
- How to market a book when you have no followers
- Deciding whether to stick to one niche or go broad

◆ What to do when all your content is underperforming

And a *lot* more. I'll be tying in the concepts I talked about in this book, and even touching some marketing strategies that go beyond social media.

Let me know which of the following scenarios resonated with you the most @garyvee on X (Twitter).

You're a young person who wants to join your family business, which is a roofing company in a small town. You know you can bring value by exploding your family business's organic social content. Your parents (who currently run the business and all the marketing) are skeptical about trying out your ideas and want to stick to their current strategy which predominantly involves local SEO. You want to prove to them that organic social can work and actually drive sales for the company—what would you do first?

If you know my family business origin story, you know I have a lot of passion and a lot of ideas for this.

Here's my very direct plan of attack that will work for many, and I look forward to getting lots of emails (gary @vaynerx.com) of success stories with this strategy:

Step 1: Create brand-new accounts on social media related to your business category. In this scenario, I'd create handles like @dailyroofing or @roofingtips. By starting with these accounts, you won't "screw up" or "bother" the way the train is running at the company. Your parents who are skeptical about your strategies might not let you run the main social media handles for the company, but chances are they won't mind if you create new handles from scratch. That'll give you the option to try different things and do goofy stuff that isn't "on brand" or "what they're used to."

Even if you can't run the main accounts associated with your family business—no excuses. You can create accounts like @roofingdaily.

But be careful. The number one mistake in this scenario is this: Kids just want to do things for the sake of doing them. They want to say their parents or uncles are "old" and don't get it. What they don't realize is, most social media content doesn't lead to direct sales results immediately. Don't talk a big game to your parents, uncles, or grandparents—tell them that this will take years to build, so that if you do have a post that gets a lot of views and leads to a couple of clients, it's considered an early indication of success. If you talk a big game up front, you dig yourself into a hole if or when the content underdelivers.

Step 2: Make sure you're following the strategies in this book. After you get your account usernames, make sure that the profiles are set up properly with the right phone number or email. Make sure you know who you're ideating content for (create cohorts). Research Reddit, Quora, and other platforms to find common questions people have about roofing. Search terms like "roofing tips" on TikTok and Facebook and see what content styles and formats are most popular and try to replicate those.

For a genre like roofing, every platform is in play—from LinkedIn to TikTok. But you need to follow the modern advertising framework. Create different content for different platforms based on different consumer psychologies.

You have a business that solves immediate, urgent problems that people have (for example, a locksmith). Most of your customers come through SEO and SEM, since people often search "locksmith in [your city]" when they need your services. You're not sure how content and social media can help drive sales for your business as you won't be reaching customers in their time of need. What would your social media strategy look like?

First off, understand that social media search is aggressively on the rise. It's no different than placing an ad on Google or maximizing your website to show up higher on Google search rankings. Content on social media can achieve the same effect. There will always be people who need a locksmith for the first time, and many of them will be under the age of thirty. They'll go to TikTok or Instagram search in addition to places like Google. If the content you put out is optimized properly, there's a chance you'll show up higher in search on social platforms. In the coming years with AI, the search game is about to change even more as people search with chatbots, not just search engines.

I think locksmiths could still benefit from posting fifty, sixty, or seventy meaningful pieces of how-to content across social platforms and informative content related to their field. The reality is, you're one overperforming post away from getting a ton of awareness, but more importantly, you're preparing yourself to be a relevant marketer. If you're retiring as a locksmith in the next three to four years, I understand. But if you're planning on doing it longer, consumer behavior is moving quickly away from *just* traditional Google search in the same way that it was moving quickly away from the yellow pages in the late 1990s and early 2000s.

What I'm saying in this book right now is the same thing I was saying to locksmiths in the late 1990s who thought they didn't need to have a website and thought that having placement in the yellow pages was the strategy. It's okay to stick to your "tried and true" approach, but always build out the "next." Searching on social media for "time of need" services is a trend that will not slow down.

By the way, if I were a locksmith today, I would make a lot of content on how not to hire a locksmith. Show people a couple of little things they can do to solve their problem that they can do without you. It creates reputation and trust, and ironically leads to more business, not less. People like holding on to their secrets; they think that's how you make the money. The truth is, building reputation and brand is how you make your money.

You're the marketing lead for a B2B SaaS company that sells to senior executives at large organizations. You're tasked with generating leads for the sales team. You're building out an organic social media strategy, but your sales team and the rest of your colleagues are skeptical that content can drive qualified leads. How would you begin setting up a strategy that works?

LinkedIn, LinkedIn, LinkedIn, LinkedIn, LinkedIn.

LinkedIn right now is one of the most exciting platforms when it comes to organic content. It is incredibly contextual to the B2B environment. Consumers are in a "business" mindset when they're on LinkedIn. As I mentioned before, the same person consuming content on Instagram would have a slightly different mindset when they're on LinkedIn (or any other platform for that matter), which would lead to different opportunities for relevance and driving leads.

In this situation, you shouldn't waste time trying to convince your chief financial officer or head of sales that your LinkedIn strategy will work—they won't believe it.

What you need to do is refine your talents and get really good at paid advertising and organic LinkedIn strategy. What you must also do—and this is key—is create a black-and-white measurable lead-generation framework. Meaning, you must create an original email that doesn't exist in the organization anywhere else, and/or an original phone number that's not used anywhere else. This way, you can make sure to add that contact info to your LinkedIn page or profile, so that you have clear attribution for leads that are coming through LinkedIn versus other channels. You don't want other departments to take credit for what you and your team have done.

Create two to five pieces of creative a day for LinkedIn, minimum, to post organically. When certain posts overperform, convert those into paid ads with a sales focus. Remember that LinkedIn offers the opportunity to target very ag-

gressively through their ad product; you can run ads to employees of organizations that you want to sell to, which means you can contextualize your creative to that specific organization. The more relevant the content is to the person that's seeing it, the more likely they're going to convert. This is why the same modern advertising framework in this book applies to B2B just like B2C—put out a high volume of content so you can find what's relevant, run that content as an ad, and increase your chances of converting.

From a creative format standpoint, doing green screen videos can work quite well. You could screenshot a press release or an article written about your product in, say, a B2B magazine and have a technical leader from the company add commentary on top of it. This is exciting for a couple of reasons:

1. It creates excitement among the employee base, as employees see fellow team members in the content.
2. It shows a deeper depth of knowledge that may be intriguing to potential customers on the other side. If you have an engineer or a data scientist add commentary, it helps show how

smart the team is and the thought that went into the product.

When you're making content in the B2B world, it's important to remember that you're not playing the same game as B2C. Meaning, companies like Nike, PepsiCo, and Bose are going to get a lot more views and engagement than, say, B2B SaaS pharmaceutical companies.* Don't be discouraged by lower view counts—in B2B, what matters is getting a few high-value customers to see your content.

In B2B, even if you get ten people engaging with your content, you might be able to get one or two to convert, which makes the entire marketing plan ROI positive. That's different from a B2C company that might get 10,000 views on their content but might only get one small customer from that.

To summarize this one, putting out relevant content on LinkedIn and running ads is the game. Put out stuff that's engaging and genuinely valuable, in addition to content that's more sales-oriented, asking people to sign up.

You're a successful entrepreneur who wants to shift your focus toward angel investing. You have a significant amount of capital, but you don't have access to investment opportunities. You want to showcase your expertise and want to attract more companies that will let you invest. What platforms would you prioritize, and what would your content strategy look like?

In this scenario, I would put out content analyzing current startups.

Oftentimes, the biggest opportunity in the world is to do the work before you're paid for it. If you want to work in marketing, go out and produce content where you show how you would do marketing for brands. If you want to be an angel investor, you can make content based on what skill sets you bring to the table as an investor; if you want to advise companies with their operations, for example, make videos about that. You can also make videos analyzing startups from Crunchbase, AngelList, or other businesses you're familiar with.

---

* Full disclosure: PepsiCo and Bose are VaynerMedia clients.

Start by downloading the apps, visiting websites, and analyzing the companies as an investor would analyze them. This is what I did. My angel investing career started with my observations of the current startups that were making noise. I would argue one of the reasons I invested in Facebook and X (Twitter) is that I made a video lying on a couch that was called "Facebook should be worried about Twitter." I'm giving you advice that I've taken myself.

Start by making videos. If you're not good at video, write detailed analysis in written form on LinkedIn, or use the notes app to type out your thoughts. You could also display the text over, say, a five-slide carousel on Instagram and TikTok with music playing in the background. Use the creative styles and formats from part 5 of this book.

If you're good at your analysis, your content will find its way to smart people, including the founders of those companies (especially companies that are less than six months old, because they're happy anyone is talking about their company at that point). That will lead to your opportunities.

You're a creator on TikTok who has built a following based on "owning a trend." In other words, you've posted many similar videos with the same format and style that have gotten traction because people find them funny. You frequently get a lot of views on your videos, and now you're trying to figure out a strategy to monetize that attention. What would you do?

There are a couple of things that come to mind in this scenario:

1. The 80/20 rule. Continue to do the standard content you're already doing 80 percent of the time, but 20 percent of the time challenge yourself to do something completely different. That's two out of ten posts where you should be switching things up and making content about something you normally don't. It is highly likely that you'll get far fewer views and less engagement; however, on the nineteenth time you do it, you might find your next big "thing." If you never try to put out different stuff, you'll never find it, and

I have watched hundreds of thousands of influencers and creators get into ruts and lose their place in the game because they never added the 20 percent.

2. I would think about every business on earth that could possibly want the attention of the audience that you've amassed. If your content typically is around humor, you know every comedy club wants to sell tickets. Every streaming service wants people to watch their new comedy special. There are unlimited apparel brands who would be willing to align with a comedy-centric marketing approach.

It is your job to reach out to those businesses as much as it is those businesses' jobs to find you in the wild and reach out to you. Too many creative people are incapable of selling, which is fine—this is why you get managers, agents, and business partners. But if you're asking me what I would do, I would reach out to organizations and ask them if they want to partner. There is nothing off-putting about respectfully reaching out via direct message or email to companies to make them aware of what you're up to, especially if you enjoy those products and services.

Diversify your content and start reaching out to brands to partner with them.

You're a working professional who's lived in your town for years, with a strong passion for politics and ideas for what should be changed in your local area, but you have zero political experience. You're charismatic and you're a great leader in your field, so you have a sense that you can do this. You want to run for mayor against the local incumbent, but few people know who you are outside of your colleagues and your friends, and you don't have a lot of money to throw into a campaign. What would you do?

Facebook, Facebook, Facebook, Facebook.

I believe Facebook is an incredibly strong platform, especially for localized initiatives—whether it's a local business, local political issues, or anything else. For me, the starting point here would be going live on Facebook to do virtual "town halls," posting at scale locally, and running ads ($20–$30 at a time) sharing your opinions with the local area. If it were me, I would do all that before I even announce that I'm running for mayor.

You could take anywhere between five to twelve of your biggest issues, from hard-hitting serious ones to lightweight ones, and make content around them. It could range from issues you have with the school system to the pothole down on Main Street that you're going to fix and everything in between. Post content on your Facebook page, see what is over-performing, and run those as ads to the people who live in your town.

It doesn't take a lot of money to run ads to local zip codes. You can run ads for $50–$100 apiece and see results if your content is good enough. Since you're running the ad in a local town, there would be natural shareability—people would pass the content around to each other. You'll quickly get a sense if there's any interest or validity in your platform or the issues you're talking about, which could inform your greater political campaign strategy. List forty to fifty topics you want to campaign against, post about them, run $100 worth of ads to amplify that content, and then decide which six topics will make up the foundation of your political campaign based on the comments and overall analytics.

Obviously all the other social media platforms matter too, but you need to be "eyes wide open" about politics. What I mean by that is this: One of the reasons I like Facebook is that it skews older. The reality is, the older demographic tends to vote more, so I believe Facebook is a very fertile ground for politics.

Another thing to consider when making content is, how can you create a strategy that lets you build your campaign, and make content at the same time? For example, the reason I do public speaking is to 1) serve the audience that's listening in-crowd, and 2) film the speech to make content after the fact.

In this scenario, I'd literally knock on every door in town, for the same two reasons:

1. Knocking on doors still works more than people realize. I would spend 7 a.m. to 10 p.m. knocking on every door, talking to every single citizen in the town. I mean all of them.
2. It would be the foundation of my content machine. Film everything, and postproduce the most interesting interactions for social media content and run that content as ads in the local area.

I believe that what I'm writing in this scenario will become a foundational framework for many local politicians to win local elections, and I look forward to future leaders in politics emailing me about these exact pages.

You're the CMO of a major consumer packaged goods (CPG) brand selling cleaning products, and you've been hearing about the potential of TikTok skits to drive demand around your product. Your brand has a mascot, and you're trying to figure out how to use it for these skits. How would you begin coming up with ideas and what would be your strategy to start your company's experimentations in this area?

For examples of how to incorporate mascots into your content, you can go look at Duolingo.* You can go look at @goodboy.noah on TikTok.

I think the Fortune 500 advertising world has gotten a little too predictable and professional, and gone away from certain things that have worked quite well. In the 1950s, '60s, and '70s, advertising was littered with mascots that really drove in-credible sales—we have examples like the Marlboro Man, the Pillsbury Doughboy, the Jolly Green Giant, and much, much more. We have a much stronger affinity toward content with mascots compared to content without them. I believe that the current form of social media will be the reigniter of more mascot usage in Madison Avenue ad-land.

This is not just for Fortune 500 com-panies; I would argue that a lot of small businesses should be getting more seri-ous about creating a mascot. They should create a character in a mascot costume doing stuff in their little ice cream store, bike shop, or auto repair shop. In fact, I would argue that the rise of influencer marketing and personalities behind businesses like "GaryVee" are kind of like "mascots," which is why it works so well. I'm especially bullish on mascots as a strategy for all the introverted execu-tives who are reading this right now, not just the Fortune 500 set. It's an opportu-nity to have a character be the face of the brand, rather than a human being.

When you're experimenting with mas-cots, make sure to let the mascot have a

---

* Full disclosure: VaynerMedia works with Duolingo in Latin America.

lot of flexibility in their personality. Consider having multiple ones, so you can create fun interactions between them.

For Fortune 500 chief marketing officers, social media is a safe place to "test" a mascot. Since social media still doesn't feel "official" in the advertising world (even though it's the most official to me), it's a good place to test how people respond to different mascot characters over the course of a few months or a year. You could start with using face filters over your product so that it can "talk" (for example, at the time of writing, TikTok has an effect that can layer on eyes and a mouth over an item). You can include it in different trends and stories, and see what character attributes viewers respond to best. From there, you can round out the character of your mascot and potentially turn it into a cartoon, a real-life puppet, a costume that someone wears, or a number of other options.

If the mascot doesn't hit, you can kill the mascot and start another one. If it *does* hit, you can integrate it in national campaigns or a Super Bowl commercial, or put the mascot in outdoor media campaigns.

I also think businesses should consider having the mascot interact with the founder or another executive from the company; it's another fun way to humanize the individuals behind the brand.

You're a marketing leader at a large brand that wants to advertise in new categories, such as esports. You want to make sure that your marketing and collaborations feel authentic, rather than just advertising for the sake of advertising. How would you think through your strategy to do that?

I would put in about fifty hours of research into any category I was looking to get into. With a category like esports, I would dedicate hours either through myself, my team, or my agency partners to understand the current state of the industry. For example, it's important to understand that the professional *Fortnite* player known as Clix is potentially more culturally relevant within the esports world at the time of writing compared to Ninja, who has been a dominant figure in the industry for years.* It's important

---

* Full disclosure: VaynerSports represents Clix.

to understand the state of the union of *Fortnite, Call of Duty,* and what's going through people's minds about various influencers and games. Understand what's currently the most relevant, and which influencers, games, and platforms have the audiences that would be meaningful to your brand. Search esports lingo and read comments from the few dozen esports accounts that matter the most in culture to get a sense for the market overall. Understand the slang, the inside jokes, what only the hard-core fans would know that no one else knows. All this knowledge will make you a better decision maker for what campaigns you need to execute, and it will help you evaluate campaigns for your partners.

Do the listening work before the execution because that's the stuff that truly matters. Otherwise, you risk making partnerships that don't make sense and coming off as inauthentic.

You've built a substantial audience on YouTube through your "how-to" skin-care-related videos. However, you've recently reignited your childhood passion for music. You want to talk more about the world of music and different artists (potentially even

make your own), but you're not sure whether to start a completely different channel for this or post it on the same channel as your skin-care videos. What would you do?

Creators and influencers often worry about losing their current audience when they're going after their happiness or the next opportunity that they see. I think it's a huge mistake.

I went through this. I broke out as a wine content producer with *Wine Library TV,* but later I wanted to make business content because that was what was in my heart. Plenty of my wine audience didn't come along with me on my new journey. Plenty of them said what most content creators fear the most: something along the lines of "I'm not watching your wine show anymore and I'm not buying wine from your dad's store anymore because I'm upset that you're making business content." That actually happened.

Obviously, it ended up being a good decision. And even if it didn't end up being a good decision financially or professionally, it still would have been right because living for others is always a bad decision. In this scenario, if you resist putting out music content because your audience only wants to see skin-care content, you will begin to resent your audience over time. Instead of choosing between music or skin care, you can do both. Good news: The new social media world allows this to happen.

Let me explain.

With the TikTokification of social media, you could have three followers on TikTok and post tomorrow and if your content is good, you can miraculously have 100,000 people seeing that video. Your content will "find" its audience. Same in this scenario. If you've historically been a makeup person but your first video about music is amazing, then you might find more people will see it, not less. You just need to be mentally ready for some of your existing followers criticizing you.

The bottom line is, don't stop yourself from posting just because you think it's not going to get likes or you'll lose followers. That's never a winning formula. To remind you, I post about garage sales, business talk, mindset, VeeFriends, the New York Jets, and it all works. That doesn't mean that every piece of content is going to do great, but overall, you'll find your cadence and some stuff will hit. A video I made about my love for blueberries was one of my most successful posts of all time, and that wouldn't have made any sense to anyone, including me at the time.

Be your most true and authentic self, and you will be happier. If you take that path, there's a very high likelihood that you'll be more professionally successful in the long term. That's the way I see it.

You have a small investment management firm that's been in business for many years, running primarily on word-of-mouth referrals. You started playing around with LinkedIn content during the COVID time period as you couldn't see your clients, so you've managed to build a small following there, but don't have a presence anywhere else. Your primary goal is to sell your practice in the next five years and retire, and you're trying to plan your overall content strategy around that. What would you do?

LinkedIn is going to be imperative here. The secondary platform I would consider is YouTube, both long-form videos and Shorts.

If I were in this scenario, I would start a weekly, biweekly, or, at minimum, a monthly podcast. I would interview founders, other fund managers, and other private equity firms in the context of investing. You can also make a list of the firms that you think might buy your firm and invite those partners or soon-to-be partners to be guests on your podcast. Not only is it a good way to make content that would be relevant to prospective buyers, but it's also a way to build relationships with those individuals who might consider buying your firm themselves down the road.

You'd be surprised how many big names in your industry would say yes to being on your podcast even though your podcast has no traction. Many people just enjoy the process of telling their stories, and even though you'll get forty-nine nos for every fifty requests, that one yes will be meaningful.

You'll have to grind on cold emails and LinkedIn. As you're doing this, make sure you don't annoy people. Don't hit them up fifteen times but try to cast a wide net while being respectful—even if you don't get the biggest name in your space, you might be able to get someone with a fascinating story or personality, and that could be the clip that reaches prospective buyers on LinkedIn.

Once you get a few people who say yes, do a forty-five-minute podcast with each of them and post each episode as a long-form YouTube video. Of course, chop up clips from that long-form video and distribute them across social media with a special focus on LinkedIn and YouTube Shorts.

When you do see organic posts that overperform your average, take those clips and run them as ads targeting firms that you think are most likely to buy your firm. For B2B companies especially, I think this is a strategy more people need to consider—create ads specifically for employees of companies that you want to buy your product or firm. It's one of the underrated tactics in the B2B world, something that holds a lot of opportunity.

Your business has a common product that everybody could use. Prior to reading this book, your content consisted of broad videos that were meant to appeal to everyone, but now you're considering more specific cohorts to target. However, with limited content creation resources, you're not sure how to choose what cohorts to prioritize so that you see higher return on investment, compared to making a few pieces of content for everyone. What would you do?

The first thing I would do is audit every single one of my expenses.

Maybe your travel and entertainment budget (the flights you take and the client dinners you have) is too high. Maybe you've done the same trade show three times already, and you can have a smaller booth instead of a large one. Maybe two of your eleven employees aren't great, and you need to help your bottom performers move on and find different jobs. It's essential to focus on finding as many dollars for content creation as possible.

Marketing grows businesses, and too many businesses don't allocate much energy or money to their marketing. Especially for the smaller businesses and entrepreneurs, instead of cutting two employees, maybe you could live a slightly less lavish lifestyle and take home $150,000 a year instead of $200,000 and pour that $50,000 back into your business so that you can take home $300,000 in a few years. There's never a bad time to invest in a good business.

That is the first thing I would do.

When it comes to prioritizing cohorts,

I would look at places where the business has historically done well. If moms ages 25–35 in Houston have previously bought in high volume, that could become a cohort you double down on and you could go narrower there. Beyond that, you could look at other cohorts that you believe you could win over if you marketed with more "teeth." If you feel that your product should be doing better with teenage boys, maybe you make content for 15–19-year-old Middle America gamers as the target and distribute that on Snapchat and TikTok.

Even if you have a broad product like a beverage or an apparel brand, creating a high volume of narrow cohorts would give you a much better chance at increasing relevance (which increases sales).

You're a CMO of a company that has traditionally focused on B2B software sales, and you've developed a solid reputation in the market. Your company is now branching into the B2C market with a new product line. You want to create a marketing strategy to appeal to individual consumers without compromising your established B2B relationships. What would you do?

Realize that there's little to no risk of compromising the relationship.

There are many tech companies, like Microsoft, Google, and others, that have heavy B2B and B2C components that co-exist. You can market to different demographics within the same business. It's okay.

In general, the biggest issue in marketing today is that companies believe in "or" instead of "and." They think they need to choose which cohorts to market to, instead of making relevant content for many different cohorts. By making relevant creative for many different consumer segmentations on your B2C product, there's not going to be a B2B buyer seeing that ad on Instagram thinking, "Oh, this company is silly. Let's undo all our B2B infrastructure because they made a relevant ad."

It is a fear-based ideology that is overly conservative, tone-deaf, and grounded in outdated academic textbooks. It's crazy to think that advertising that is relevant to someone is going to be detrimental to your business, unless you're posting highly polarizing content. If you are a very high-end brand and you make content that's relevant to the middle class, you're not going to lose as many of your consumers as you think. In fact, if that were true, all the biggest fashion brands wouldn't have done all these collaborations with all the streetwear brands that actually made the high-end brands more relevant, not the other way around.

Stop being scared. Make content that's relevant for different people. Different people are going to buy your T-shirt or software or shoes, and they're going to buy them for different reasons. There's so much fear around being "on brand" that prevents companies from being relevant. People have chosen vanilla messaging to one group because they fear being relevant to every group, and it's limiting their growth.

If you're only selling vanilla, your customers are only going to be people who like vanilla. If you're selling different flavors that various people like, you're going to have more people buying. It's just business. This "academia"-based marketing that the Fortune 500 has been executing for the last three decades is a pandemic.

You're starting to experiment with putting out more of your personal content on social media and sharing your personal story instead of just your business. You want to talk about your backstory and share advice, but you don't want to come off as too egotistical when talking about yourself. How will you share your story while keeping that balance in mind?

It is not very hard to balance talking about topics that you're proud of while also talking about topics you're less proud of or things you've struggled with. I often talk about my origin story with pride, but I also mix in the fact that I wasn't a good student. I talk about peeing in my bed until I was eleven. I mix in my struggles with being in a family business, and the opportunities I missed, such as passing on Uber in the angel round.

Being egotistical is a personality trait grounded in insecurity. That has nothing to do with telling your own story. In fact, as I write this, I'm sitting with Sid, Dustin, and Raghav on my team, three people I've worked with closely for a long time. I've heard them talk about themselves often; they've all easily figured out how to not be egotistical. As a matter of fact, I think they're sometimes too humble. It's not hard to do this.

The act of telling your story doesn't automatically mean that you're coming from a place of ego. I know many of us are taught to not talk about ourselves, but

why is that bad? How are you supposed to talk about your hobbies or something that genuinely makes you proud without feeling proud? I don't understand the concept of not speaking the truth.

Of course, sometimes you might really be into what you're saying, and that passion might come off as ego, but that's just a misinterpretation. We're just people; we're just talking. I'm proud of the things I've done in business. I don't think that's bragging. I think that's just my story. It's what happened.

The context is important too. If you went up onstage and your keynote was just "I'm really attractive!" and then you immediately left, then yes that might be perceived as egotistical. But if you said, "I grew up very attractive. Let me tell you what that meant. Here are the good things that came from it, here are the negative things that came from it," then that becomes a completely different story. It's what I do in my content and even this book—I talk about how I took advantage of tools like email marketing and Google AdWords early, but I use those stories to set up all the value I'm trying to provide.

You're the CMO of a large vodka brand that is trying to reposition itself to a luxury brand rather than just another vodka. How would you use the strategies in this book and other marketing strategies to go about doing that?

The first thing I would do in this scenario is see if you even have the permission to do that.

If you're trying to reposition your brand as luxury, the first issue is the price of the product, not necessarily the marketing. If you're not priced like a luxury item, do you have the capacity to raise the price? If not, it'll be hard to change your brand's positioning no matter what kind of marketing you do.

No matter how good Gucci's marketing is, if Gucci bags and clothes were 80 percent cheaper than they are today, they'd struggle to maintain their luxury image. With a lower price tag, Gucci might fall into a chic, cool, well-priced brand category almost like Tito's Vodka is positioned in the vodka category, but it wouldn't be high-end luxury.

If you want to play in a high-end world, you'll have to change the price, which is challenging. It's hard to go from being a $30 bottle of vodka to a $60 bottle of vodka when everybody used to buy you for $30.

Don't forget, marketing is a *partner* in building a business; it's not the only variable that exists. In this scenario, there's some business talk that needs to happen first before you even get to the marketing point.

If you're just looking to elevate the brand's positioning slightly to what I call "affordable luxury," then that's more doable. There are many brands that we all know of that feel a little bougie but aren't that expensive. I would argue that Nike's Air Force Ones have been able to achieve this—you can buy a regular pair of Air Force Ones for somewhere around $80–$200. That's not inexpensive by any measure, but unless you're looking at the rare ones, you won't have to pay $500–$1,000+ like some luxury shoe brands cost.

If a vodka brand wanted to reposition itself without raising the price, I would focus on what the brand is associated with through creative content. It's kind of like reinventing your image in college after graduating from high school (which is harder in today's social media world, but much easier in my generation's world, when strangers had no way of knowing who you were). The reinvention required doing different things—you had to wear different clothes, different words had to come out of your mouth, you had to hang out with different people, and more.

Same for marketing. If you were putting out content with twenty-three-year-old kids playing beer pong and watching football after work, that's how people will think of your vodka. Here's what you could do instead if you wanted to reposition:

Take a picture of the bottle in a polo match in the Hamptons instead of in a college dorm room. Work, for example, with an influencer like Michael B. Jordan, who is well-dressed like a model, instead of an influencer from Barstool. Post a picture of a martini cocktail at, say, Carbone's private club instead of your vodka on a picnic table among twenty-five-year-olds in Central Park.

With new content, you're showing the world that your brand is playing at a different level.

Still, this is not an easy task, especially if you're an established brand. But there have been many brands that have been able to elevate to different levels of prestige when not originally positioned that way. Nike, for example, started out as just a utilitarian running shoe, and ended up being able to sell $2,000 sneakers as

well. You do that by storytelling around the brand in a different way; you need to act the part if you want to reposition the brand through its creative, imagery, and the events you're sponsoring.

By the way, if the world has taught us anything in the last twenty years, it's that what is "high-end" gets redefined often. Today a forty-five-year-old businessperson is more likely to wear a high-fashion hoodie or baseball cap than a business suit with ties or Italian shoes. Some of the examples above are what may be happening now, but keeping an eye on how pop culture is evolving and what the top 10 percent of earners are doing may allow you to jump on certain trends around the redefining of the upper class at affordable rates. These are big "land grab" opportunities.

You've built a following as a creator on multiple platforms around your love for fashion. You have a small community, and you want to partner with more clothing brands to earn more money from sponsored work. You've done a few partnerships where you've done posts for brands in exchange for free products, but you want to grow into someone that can charge for promotion. What would you do?

This is a big game of, If you don't ask, you don't get.

In this scenario, you've been happy with posting stuff that people sent you for free because that was cool for you. A year ago, or six months ago or two years ago, you didn't get free clothes, and getting free stuff seemed pretty rad. Today you feel like you're ready to take the next step because you've been growing. So going forward, every time a brand reaches out to you or says they like your stuff, when they engage in looking to do a deal, you explain to them that you will not post just for product when they ask; you have a fee. Ask for money. It's that simple.

For a lot of people, the concept of asking for money is a challenge. It's not how they were brought up; it's not in their DNA. But this scenario is easy—it's about getting to a place where you're comfortable asking.

The more interesting question here is, if they said no, would you still want to do it for the free clothes? If so, you should be prepared to come back with your tail between your legs, and say, "On second thought, I think your stuff is so fantas-

tic that I will do it in exchange for your products." Then you should be prepared for them to say no because sometimes they'll be salty after you ask for money. You have to be okay with that.

If you keep building your brand, if you keep building an audience, if you keep posting content, you will find brands that will give you actual money. Every time you engage in a negotiation with brands on DMs and on the phone, consider offering different proposals: It could be a combination of accepting free stuff as well as money, asking for more money per post, asking for even more money the following time, asking for a high minimum amount of posts to do a "series," or even allowing for one post at a higher fee because you don't want to clog your feed. Make sure you're always mixing different proposals for different prices, so that after you do that a couple of dozen times, you have a good sense of what your market opportunity is.

You're a thought leader in your field with a book coming out in the next several months. You've been somewhat active on social media, but you don't have a huge community, and you don't often get meaningful engagement on your posts yet. You're trying to find the best short-term strategies to boost book sales without needing to rely on your current organic social following or your email list. What would you do?

Short-term strategies scare the crap out of me. If you're in this situation, understand that anything you do short-term is going to feel more transactional and salesy. I'm hoping that the people in this scenario are two years away from writing a book versus two months from writing a book because they're going to have a much better chance of achieving what they want.

That said, in this scenario I would message every single podcaster or video blogger asking for an interview—starting with the people who reach the audience your book is for, and scaling from there. You'll want to cast a wide net as a lot of people won't respond, so try to aim for 17 out of 297 or 13 out of 567 requests.

Once you get on those podcasts, take the clips from those interviews and distribute them across your social channels.

Attention is the currency that will lead people to consider your book. If you have not amassed your own attention, you

have to rent it from others. It's the same reason people used to go on *The Howard Stern Show*, *The Today Show*, MTV, or QVC to try to sell their product.

Because you don't have a big platform in this scenario, you're probably not the number one choice for someone like Joe Rogan or any other top podcast. So you'll have to find mid-tier and smaller shows with the goal of trading on volume. In other words, doing a bunch of small podcasts could add up to being on a bigger podcast. That's your best option here.

Realize that you need to be following the framework of this book now, which would then give you the leverage in three to six years or so to accomplish what you want, whether that's running for mayor or selling a book or anything else. If you don't amass your own attention, you become a beggar, and beggars can't be choosers. I hope this inspires people who have big ambitions two, four, six, eight years out to start doing it now because the days of "short-term" campaigns and "short-term strategies" to create meaningful outcomes are getting harder and more expensive.

A shout-out to Raghav, who helped me with this book and my last one. After I got done with that whole rant above, he said to me, "What about trends on Tik-Tok that go viral and generate sales?"

My answer to that is, yes, there will always be instances where content can take off short-term. You might get lucky. But *lucky* is the word. You might make a single video with the hashtag #booktok on TikTok, which goes viral and launches your book into the bestseller category. Like I mentioned in the introduction of this book, a young woman made a video about a dad who wrote a book years ago, and her video turned that book into a bestseller. It can happen. You can get lucky too. But luck is not a strategy.

You've been putting out content for a while on a platform, but in recent weeks, you've seen numbers on all your content decrease. You're unsure of whether you got shadow-banned, whether your content just isn't as good anymore, or whether the platform isn't working as well anymore. How would you uncover the core problem here?

This is one of the most common questions I get asked and I believe it's secretly the most common question that people want to ask.

The reality is, 99.99 percent of you need to get out of this concept of "shadow banning." I heard people refer to this term a lot around 2017–18, as the supply of content on Instagram increased and organic reach began to decline for some major influencers. They wanted to blame the platform, not realizing they were starting to lose market share because of the game of supply and demand.

The reason I was yelling at the top of my lungs about TikTok in 2019 was that I realized that demand for content was there, but the supply of content wasn't. Most of you—influencers, creators, small businesses, corporations—were just enjoying executing on Instagram, and you weren't willing to move quickly on Tik-Tok. That was the mistake, and that was the opportunity. Today TikTok is already different. It's harder to make a video get 5–10 million views on TikTok today, whereas years ago it was more common. Why? Because now more people are posting on TikTok and the supply of content is higher.

That's the way it will always work. The answer to your question is, you need to make new stuff. It's the purpose of this whole book. Maybe by giving your cohorts more "teeth," you will make more relevant content, which then gets your content more reach. Use different adjectives, use different analogies, make different styles and formats of videos, use different kinds of pictures or words in the copy.

If you normally post videos, try a carousel. Analyze your first three seconds and see if there's any fluff in your content there that can be cut out. If you're in every video, maybe you don't need to be—maybe that will lead to more shareability beyond just your existing audience.

You just need to push yourself to make your creative look different.

You're an executive at a regional restaurant chain that has dozens of locations, each run by franchisees. You're noticing that some franchisees are starting social accounts for their own stores, with differing levels of content "quality" and different ways of portraying the brand. You're trying to decide what you should allow and what you shouldn't. What would you do?

Boy oh boy, is this a hornet's nest.

The franchisor-franchisee dynamic is one of the most interesting ones in business today. Obviously if you know this model, the franchisee is already kicking a certain percentage of their sales to the franchisor to do overall marketing. Many franchisees are frustrated that they don't have enough localized advertising going on, which is why they're getting into this issue.

The franchisor, on the other hand, is worried about whether marketing is on brand.

This is what I'd say:

For the franchisees locally, remember that you decided to be a franchisee. If you wanted to have full control, you could have started your own entrepreneurial business and not rely on all the things the franchisor does. So, accept what they're doing with their marketing budget, but feel comfortable in doing your own marketing according to what's allowed by your bylaws. Make it more localized but have empathy that the franchisor has concerns around their brand.

I'll say it nice and slow: You signed up to be a franchisee. You could have not done so. There are many local restaurants, for example, and local gyms. In this situation, you have to follow the bylaws that are in your agreement.

On the franchisor part, you should approach the situation with empathy. Even though they signed up to be a franchisee, as long as the franchisee isn't doing anything egregiously bad (such as undermining pricing strategies or posting highly polarizing content), you need to get off your corporate high horse and stop saying that it's off brand. The content they're sharing might be very on brand locally. Depending on where the store location is, it might be more urban, or more country, or closer to college or different dynamics, so you need to lay off the pedal a little bit.

That's my recommendation. Much like parenting, in this situation I prefer to talk in generalizations because everybody really knows their kids best. I'm aware that what I just laid out is very on the nose because I live in this world; however, I'm empathetic that there may be different dynamics at play. Everyone needs to walk with "eyes wide open." I'll forever be somebody who supports localized and contextual creative. The more vanilla it is, the more likely it's not going to do well. The more corporate and global it is, the more likely it's vanilla. I always prefer to give local markets as much leeway as possible because they know how to make it most contextual.

You're a C-suite leader at a major brand, and you know that you can help your company by putting out your own content on LinkedIn and other platforms. What would be your approach to kick this off?

First, I would speak to the stakeholders internally in HR, legal, and the C-suite to make sure they're okay with it because that's just the reality of the situation. But if this is you, you're on the right track. You've got the right hunch.

At VaynerX, we've seen it—building brands of executives through social is a massive breakthrough for most corporations, especially in the B2B space. I emphatically recommend that all executives take this very seriously because it's good for business, and it's good for you.

Especially on LinkedIn, a front-facing human being can "warm up" the logo. We've seen remarkable opportunities for business development because of it. For B2B organizations, it leads to much higher lead generation.

For the individuals in this situation, it's also a good hedge. The reality is, corporations do lay people off. The more you put yourself out there, the more likely it is that you'll land on your feet. Obviously sometimes there's a direct conflict here and the corporation might feel that this concept is too self-promotional, since they don't want you to be recruited and go somewhere else. I respect that, I understand that, and I recommend starting off talking to the stakeholders and understanding whether the organization supports somebody being out in front of the logo or if they're against it.

If a business fears losing an executive, a strategy you could propose is letting 15–25 senior employees and executives produce content on LinkedIn instead of one. That way, you can hedge against their concerns of one person being the face of the brand. My suggestion to boards and CEOs is to open the opportunity to a bunch of people so you're not vulnerable to one person—like a sports team isn't vulnerable to one star player.

It's very clear that human content, especially for B2B companies and Fortune 500 brands, is incredibly fertile ground for business opportunity. I couldn't recommend it more.

After looking at your customer base and your business goals, you've identified various cohorts that you want to reach based on demographics, psychographics, affinities and passions, the stage of life people are at, and more. Now you're trying to figure out what's culturally relevant for those specific groups that you've identified. As someone who's in a different age bracket and interested in different things than your cohorts, you're trying to put together a strategy to stay on top of what's relevant for each group. How would you do that?

By putting in the work.

I'm not the same age, demographic, or gender or in the same life situation of almost everybody that I market to. How do I find what's relevant to them?

I use Google Trends. I read comments on social media for an hour or two a day. I search different topics on social media based on the demographics I'm trying to learn about, which means my For You page across platforms helps me stay on top of what's happening across all those demographics. When I'm curious about a cohort, I will search their ages, what I perceive to be their interests, or what is generally known about them.

Type "teenager" into TikTok, Instagram, YouTube, and X (Twitter) and you will get a bunch of silliness. But you'll also get valuable information if you spend time sorting through it. You could read articles. You could follow certain people who might be influential in the space that you're trying to reach. There are industry leaders who are doing this research work and you can follow them on social networks and see what they're talking about. You can ask people in your life who the twenty people they follow are in different ages and demographics and start following them.

It starts with you allocating time. Everybody who's reading this has ambition. And if you have ambition, auditing your time becomes important because a lot of you are busy. You have families and you have leisure time that you need for rest and mental balance. I get it. I don't want you to add four hours of work a day. I want you to find four hours that you're wasting. For example, I believe every one of you could cut your meetings in half across the board and find the hours to dedicate to this. Personally, I mostly do fifteen-minute meetings now because I realized a decade ago that most of my thirty-minute meetings could be done in fifteen, and my one-hour meetings could be done in thirty minutes. I believe all of you have that too.

If you have ambition, maybe you don't need to take a two-hour lunch every day. Maybe it is okay for that to be an hour and you can use the resulting extra hour for research time.

But the answer here is putting in the work. Either you do it yourself or you could hire somebody, but you can't sell to consumers without knowing what they care about. The internet makes that a lot easier than focus groups in the 1970s and 1980s. Not to mention there are AI bots popping up now. Every day, apps like ChatGPT are getting better at giving you current information when you ask something like, "What are 23–27-year-old skateboarders into right now?"

You just have to actually do it.

You're an influencer who has built a following of 180,000 on Instagram from 2015 to 2023. But you missed the early TikTok boom, and you didn't establish yourself on any other platform. You're noticing that views on your Instagram Reels are going down and it's getting harder to reach your audience. What would you do?

This scenario will continue to happen over and over and over again. Platforms that are popular now will continue to evolve and will continue to either lose or gain attention.

Funny enough, as I'm writing this, a new platform called Threads, an X (Twitter) competitor coming from Meta, is on the precipice of launching and I had the opportunity to start trying it out on the Fourth of July weekend in 2023.

It's very clear to me that there are going to be many people currently reading who aren't winning on Instagram anymore, but Threads might be the platform that changes things for them. We've had platforms like Vine and Clubhouse that have had less than one year of a big run but helped establish big personalities who went on to use that moment to build elsewhere, including Swan Sit in Clubhouse, and King Bach in Vine.* Threads may go through its own ebbs and flows, and I don't know how big it's going to be, but as with any platform that has attention, it's worth taking seriously. As I'm editing this book, Threads has had its explosion, and has settled into a much less active but still meaningful social net-

work. When I think about day trading attention, there's always going to be highs and lows. Even though the macro attention on Threads right now in November 2023 is lower than it was a few months ago, the opportunity for someone reading this might be greater because most of the business and creator world has already deemed Threads as a tertiary platform (not even secondary). The dozen to a hundred people who take Threads most seriously will most likely find new audience and opportunity. In fact, some of the biggest arbitrages of growth happen on platforms like Pinterest, Snapchat, Threads, and other social networks that aren't in the top five.

Here's what I would recommend to the person in this scenario:

1. Stop crying. Just because it's not your moment, it's okay. Think about all the actors and artists (like John Travolta and Aerosmith) who have had moments when they were hot, moments when they were not, and eight years later they were hot again. I

---

* Full disclosure: VaynerSpeakers, a VaynerX company, represents Swan Sit.

would even tell you in my own career, I've had different moments when I was a little hotter or a little less hot, even though I've been very consistent with my content output. I still have ebbs and flows within my range. Just because you "missed" the TikTok boom doesn't mean you're dead forever, because even if you had hit it, that doesn't mean you'd be hot forever. Someone right now who is crushing it on TikTok might plateau as time goes on.

2. Start realizing where you're at mentally. Are you in that place to put in the work? It's important to be in the zone and at a stage where you're willing to put in the reps at the same time as the platform is having its "moment" with high organic reach.

3. Think about whether you're willing to change up your content. One of the biggest reasons people stagnate is that they put out the same types of content repeatedly. If you're in this situation, you can change up your content within Instagram, even if you don't go and find some other platform that's exploding. We're lucky that Threads is popping up right now, but it may or may not hit. The one thing you can control, whether new platforms

are emerging or declining, is your ability to change up your content. Remember, I went from wine content to business content over the course of my career. I went from very tactical business content to more mentality and strategy content, then to current events and garage-saling content. Mix up what you're putting out.

You're an affiliate marketer who has historically relied on hard, direct-response selling. You're aware that this approach won't work as well in the era of the interest graph. What would you do to change your approach around this to grow your affiliate business with the modern advertising framework?

The argument that I'm making in this book is that being good at brand building puts us in a position to be better at sales.

For affiliate marketers, I would suggest putting more effort into brand-building exercises that I speak about in this book. As long as you're linking out to your page in your bio where you have products, you can put out free content and people will look at your account and click the URL;

they can read further about what you do and potentially buy.

You can also play with new initiatives like TikTok Shop—affiliates can, at the time of writing, get commission by promoting products there.

I think of affiliate, sales-driven conversion marketing as boxing. You can only punch with your gloves in boxing, whereas this book is more like MMA, where you can use many different styles of fighting to win the match. With the modern advertising framework, you'll develop a more rounded-out marketing plan that combines various elements (including social media, experiential event activations, and running ads on streaming services, among other tactics). Now you've got boxing, jiu jitsu, and kickboxing—you're a more well-rounded fighting machine.

You're the owner of a small B2B organization that provides specialized services to businesses. You've been active on LinkedIn, and between putting out content and connecting with personal contacts, you've been able to generate new business there. You want to branch out to TikTok, Instagram, and other platforms. However, since your service is nuanced and specialized, you're worried that it's not "sexy" enough to storytell around on a platform like TikTok. How would you go about expanding beyond just LinkedIn?

I think we can all agree that if you're selling, say, insurance to large corporations, it's going to be a challenge for you to find your creative pillar on TikTok. However, I would argue that YouTube Shorts is an incredible platform for you. You could make a relevant how-to video, and title it properly; it may be exactly what your target audience is searching for.

Personally, I learn better through audio and video than from the written word, so I search a lot of nuanced business topics on YouTube to get explanations about things.

You can start by searching nuanced topics on X (Twitter) and other platforms—if you're in a specialized industry, you know the terms that people use in your world. Search those terms, find opportunities to answer questions, and make videos related to those themes for YouTube. In this situation, if the content doesn't feel right for TikTok or Instagram, I would focus more on X (Twitter), YouTube, and LinkedIn.

I would also argue that you use 5 percent of your time and resources to try out TikTok and Instagram content. Instead of sharing content about business nuances on these platforms, you could use it as an opportunity to show more of your personal side. Maybe you're a fisherman who just happens to sell concrete, shipping containers, or SaaS software, and you could put out content about your love of fishing on social platforms. What you'll find with this strategy is two things: 1) You'd give yourself a creative outlet that will teach you how to be better at social media content, and 2) you'd be stunned by how much business development can come from the videos you put out about your love for fishing, golf, chess, softball, or anything else.

Just make sure that your profile is properly set up. You could add a description like:

Fisherman
Father
[Insert a sports team you're a fan of]
Head of sales for your SaaS company

And of course, make sure your business URL is in the bio.

In this example, your core business content could be distributed on YouTube Shorts, X (Twitter), and LinkedIn, and your personal content could be distributed across TikTok, Facebook, Instagram, and Snapchat. I'm excited to get an email from a corporate executive who decided to start a TikTok account around his or her passions, and how it led to a huge sale.

After learning about post-creative strategy in this book, you're inspired to do a better job of learning from your comments. However, every time you post, you tend to get roughly the same number of comments from people telling you that they "love this post" or reacting with emojis. You're unsure of how to extract insights from comments to make your next piece of content better when the comments feel so generic. What would you do?

The best way to get insights is by asking questions through your content.

In this scenario, I would ask a direct question through my next piece of content. Let's say you have an ice cream shop. Literally in the next post, instead of showing how beautiful your ice cream is, you can ask people what flavors they like.

Maybe if the economy is tight and you have to cut two flavors, instead of guessing or even just looking at sales (which is a great indicator), another way to get more insights is by going on social media and making a video that says, "Which of these two flavors do you think we should eliminate?" You ask the question through Instagram Stories with a poll sticker overlay. You could also film yourself walking into the store, pulling out the Rocky Road flavor, and saying, "No other flavor is as good as this," which is going to make people react—maybe some will agree, maybe others will say "you're crazy, the strawberry is better." There are a lot of ways to do it.

You can also ask people what flavors they would like you to add and run that content as an ad in your local area to get more data.

Instead of just looking at your sales data (which could be skewed based on your current customer base without considering the overall opportunity of the market), you can analyze comments on your posts, which may give you a different answer and a greater sample size to look at.

After reading the sections on cohort development, SOC, PAC, modern commercials, amplification, and post-creative strategy, you want to build a team to help you execute these skills. How would you go about doing this?

Before you go about building a team, you need to know the craft.

One of the biggest issues of the last decade in social media is that a lot of businesses have built out marketing teams of kids under twenty-five because they think the "kids just get it." That's laughable. That's like saying anybody in their twenties is athletic enough to be a professional athlete. Some twenty-year-olds are truly great at modern marketing, just like some fifty-seven-year-olds are truly great at it. **This isn't about age, it's about skill.**

If you want to build out a team, put the strategies of this book into practice yourself, for months. You need to understand it in and out, so that you can hire the right people to do it for you. Otherwise, you won't know how to evaluate who's good and who's not. Even if I tell you exactly who to hire, you won't have a grasp of whether they're doing a good job. In the worst case, you'll end up paying $2,000–$5,000 a month for a marketing agency to do your content without knowing how to evaluate their performance. That doesn't mean you need to become an expert, but you do need to allocate some meaningful time over the next month or two to start dabbling so you can know enough to ask the right questions.

It's like anything else in life—even if you hire people to do your taxes and your accounting, it's not like you know nothing at all about it. You know a little bit.

When you are ready to hire, I typically recommend four main people:

1. A videographer who knows how to film and edit clips
2. A copywriter
3. A designer
4. A strategic, paid media person who has a knack for understanding the nuances of strategic organic content, platforms and culture, as well as paid media advertising.

Obviously, who you decide to hire first might change based on your priorities. Maybe to start, you hire a videographer to film your podcast and edit clips just so you can start getting some content out. You can add more layers as you get more sophisticated.

You're growing a business in a relatively small country where you're from, and you're looking to attract customers globally from different parts of the world. You feel that your country is too small for you to build a meaningful business. What would you do to scale?

Move.

. . . Okay. I'm aware that many people can't move. However, I started with that because we need to understand how in control we are. Of course, if you're born in a small country that doesn't have very good geopolitical relations, it's going to be hard to win in the new social media world. It's tough for someone in North Korea; it's tough for someone in a third world country who is incredibly poor. But the reality is, if you're in the position to read this book, you could likely move. Don't dwell in your current reality; create your new reality.

The other thing I would say is that social platforms today are global. You can make content from any part of the world. At the time of writing, the most-followed person on TikTok is Khaby Lame (@khaby.lame), who was born in

Senegal and lives in Italy. The idea that you need to "go to Hollywood" to become a major personality just isn't real anymore. With the way algorithms work, you can make content in one part of the world and have people in other countries see it, which is why it's far easier for businesses to be global. Make content for people in different parts of the world, let the algorithms serve the content globally, and watch opportunities start coming to you instead of sitting and overly focusing on the challenges no matter how significant they actually are. The biggest mistake that many in this situation make is putting their energy into what's not going well versus reallocating to what they can do about it.

You run a regional chain of beauty salons, and you've been getting new clients primarily through word of mouth, Google AdWords, and local Facebook advertising. You've been hearing about the growth that other chains have been experiencing by using influencer marketing, and you want to experiment in that strategy to grow beyond your current footprint. You want to begin putting together a strategy to research, select, and engage influencers in a way that actually leads to business results. What would you do?

Back in my Wine Library days, I often would go to my dad and say something like, "Dad, I need to try this new strategy for $10,000. There's a 99 percent chance we're going to get no return, but the learnings from it may lead to more profitability in the future."

There was never a time when I believed we would get no return, but it's a good idea to set expectations. I do it with myself to this day—whenever I try a new, innovative strategy, I pretend that there will be no return besides the learnings. That's what I would recommend to the person in this scenario. Tell yourself that the $1,000–$10,000 that you're going to budget for this is going to lead to zero return. Ironically, that mindset sets you up for greater success.

Next, let's go tactical:

To find influencers, you could start by searching your town on Instagram. I would literally open the Instagram app, hit the "search" button, and type in your town's name. Then scroll over to "tags" and click the hashtag associated with your town.

At the time of writing, there's an option to click on the hashtag and sort the results by "top posts."

Now you can start clicking around and looking at different accounts. You can look at different profiles, and contact people you might want to partner with. You could send them a direct message and say something like, "Hey, do you want to come by my salon? Let's get to know each other," or "Hey, let's grab a glass of wine." You don't necessarily have to go in for the business right away.

Or you could go in for the business if that feels more authentic for you. You could say, "Hey, I'm looking to do influencer marketing. Would you consider doing a meet-and-greet for your fans here in my salon? Does that have a cost associated with it?"

Do this with as many people as possible to learn the going rates. This will take a lot of manual hours over the course of weeks, but these are hours that you should be putting into your business. After a few weeks of talking to different influencers and meeting with them, you can try your first partnership out and learn from it. Even if the first one is a

flop, do it again. Until you have five flopping influencer marketing campaigns in your store, you shouldn't judge if it works or not.

And to remind you in this scenario, you had already heard that it does work from other salons.

The variable of success here is, are you catching someone on the "come-up" that you can get for a very good price? Can you partner with someone who can get more people to show up to your salon? The other variable is your personality. Maybe one of these influencers becomes your friend, and you create an exchange where you do their hair for free at the salon and they do posts for you for free. Or maybe the influencer has talent as an actor or actress, and you decide to shoot a few skits with them just because they might help your content overperform.

There are many different ways to make something like this work.

The biggest mistake people make here is, they overpay for someone who looks like they have a big audience but doesn't drive results. For example, if an influencer has a lot of followers but they live outside your local area, that's not going to work in this situation. In this scenario, maybe a regular person who has 2,000 followers on Instagram who looks like your target customers and lives near your store location might be better than an influencer who has a much bigger audience who doesn't live close to you. Maybe the person with 2,000 followers is an alpha, cool mom in the community and sets the trends with her friend group, which means she might generate quite a few loyal customers.

If it were me, I would try both. Test out a few posts with the highest-followed person in or near your town, and partner with a local mom or two in this scenario who might be the "alpha moms" from the parent-teacher organization who actually generate the strongest word of mouth in town.

> You're a marketing leader at a Fortune 500 company that sells a commodity product: napkins. You want to get more millennials and Gen Zers to consider your brand over competitors, but you're not sure how to differentiate. Besides putting out content and running ads, what are some unique marketing executions you would do to stand out?

The biggest thing that stands out for me with this napkin brand is marketing through apparel and merchandise. Let's break it down:

Think about some of the hoodies you see in concerts or in pop culture. One that stood out for me years back was when Blockbuster Video's logo became a popular hoodie, even though it was a store that was out of business for a while. We all know the popularity of Harley-Davidson, a motorcycle manufacturer that also has merch that people wear, or Bass Pro Shops, which created a widely popular hat. I believe more companies should consider creating merch as a form of brand marketing.

For example, if I were the brand manager of a commoditized napkin brand or a bottled-water brand, the first thing I would do (besides dominating social media creative, which is absolutely required) would be teaming up with an emerging apparel brand to do a collaboration. Brands like Madhappy and Pirate are currently emerging and gaining traction; they may be good candidates in a situation like this. Siegelman Stable is another choice (that's the hat that I've been wearing a lot, at the time of writing).* The reason for doing a collab with an emerging clothing brand rather than an established one like Kith, Rhude, or Fear of God is that you'll get even more credibility with Gen Zers and millennials who are in the "know." It's like, oh crap, this napkin brand actually gets it. Not to mention that Kith, Rhude, and Fear of God are incredibly selective and probably too expensive for most brands to collaborate with.

If people believe that a napkin brand "gets them" by doing a collab with an emerging apparel brand that they think is cool, then that brand has won "cool points." Cool points might seem silly, but it impacts how people make buying decisions. The reason brands spend millions of dollars on celebrities is to get "cool points" that will ultimately get more people to buy their products.

The cheaper, more contemporary version of this is to do a collaborative hoodie, a corduroy hat, a sock, or a T-shirt with an apparel brand that only people in the "know" know. Brands like Kith and Rhude are actually much bigger, established brands that have crossed over into mainstream (even though I'm aware there are many people reading this who have never even heard of them). That's why I suggested up-and-coming brands like Madhappy.

This resonates in a significant way with youth culture that will get them to consider and purchase your product, even if it's a commodity like a napkin, bottled water, or a toothpaste. Not to mention, people who buy your hoodies will become "billboards" because your brand will be integrated into that product. That will help you get "impressions" that are actually valuable, instead of just getting random impressions with actual billboards.

You have an emerging, premium mocktail brand. You've been putting out content and running ads, and you're wondering what else you can do to stand out from the competition in a space that's trendy. You're trying to be the dominant winner in the mocktail category, and you've got some money to invest. What would you try first?

---

* Full disclosure: I'm an investor.

In the example with the napkin brand earlier, I mentioned that I love merchandise and collaborations as marketing. Similarly, I really love the idea of event marketing as a twofer situation.

Let me explain what I mean by twofer:

Event marketing and activations at cool events like Coachella, Rolling Loud, or the Formula 1 Las Vegas Grand Prix are incredible places for this mocktail to go. This isn't new—people have been doing event marketing and sampling activations at concerts and sporting events since before I was born.

In this situation, you can combine event marketing with the modern advertising framework in this book layered on top of it.

You could set up an activation at meaningful events, and film everything that happens at your activation. You could take that four, nine, or thirty hours of film and create dozens and dozens of content pieces for social media to distribute across platforms. You're getting "two for the price of one."

Expenses-wise, you'd just have to pay for the activation, and a couple of videographers to capture everything. It's a model that way more brands should be employing—especially a mocktail, where

you'll get reactions from people who love it or compare it with other brands. It's a model that can work for most emerging consumer goods such as snacks, beverages, candies, and anything else people can consume quickly.

But just like with content, you have to be strategic about your execution at events. If you have a donut company, just handing out donuts at Coachella isn't going to work. You'd need to figure out how to make it culturally relevant to the people there. Maybe you glaze the donut with a reference to one of the biggest performers at the show, for example. Maybe you set up the activation itself with the sole purpose of capturing content. If I were setting up an activation for the GaryVee brand, I would set up a "Q&A booth" (like a kissing booth) where I answer people's questions and film it. Find versions of that for your own business.

In other words, create the activation itself with two main priorities: 1) making the activation relevant to the event and the attendees, and 2) filming everything to distribute it across social platforms.

Hey Gary, this is Sally, and my husband, Rick, and I have a question: We hear you loud and clear on the value of creative, paid media and day trading attention. We hear you on event marketing, and we hear you on merch and apparel. Give us something else that's left field, another marketing tactic under the same overall framework of day trading attention. What do you see as an emerging marketing practice that will be more widely accepted in the back half of the 2020s?

Hey Sally and Rick,

Besides social media creative, event marketing, and merchandise, I believe one of the other areas brands should be playing in is collectible products. There are many examples of this over the years:

- In 1974, Wonder Bread included a card set of Warner Bros. characters and added that to their product packaging.
- Brands like General Mills included toys in their cereal packaging for many years, such as the Cereal Squad collectible toys.
- In the mid- to late 1990s, Taco Bell included Star Wars toys with meals as new Star Wars films were released.
- McDonald's has historically done a lot of collaborations with brands like Pokémon, Disney, and Hot Wheels to include cards and toys in Happy Meals.
- Burger King has also included collectible toys in their kids' meals, often tied to popular movies or franchises.
- Hostess has included baseball cards in their packaging especially in the mid- to late 1970s—they issued a 150-card set on the bottom of snack-cake boxes.
- Cracker Jack famously included toys in their packaging for many years.*
- Special editions of Monopoly board games come with collectible tokens.
- Starbucks offers limited-edition mugs and tumblers, especially during the holiday season.
- Before they became a trading card company, Fleer included baseball cards with their gum products.
- Wheaties is known for featuring athletes on their boxes, but they've also included cutout cards on the box itself in the past.

---

* Full disclosure: Cracker Jack is operated by Frito-Lay, which is owned by PepsiCo, a VaynerMedia client.

As you can see, this is not a new concept. But the difference today is, collecting as a cultural behavior is crossing the chasm into the same realm as music, sports, and fashion.

What do I mean by that?

I believe that today—and in the back half of the 2020s—people will get together for dinner all over the world and talk about what they're currently collecting in the same way they talk about what music they're listening to, what shows they're watching, and what's going to happen this upcoming basketball season. Collecting as a behavior is starting to become "pop culture." People are getting into sneaker collecting, trading cards, NFTs, vintage clothes, and vinyl records, and not to mention the other unique items like marbles and hotel keys. More consumers are getting interested in collectibles every day, which means it's an untapped opportunity for brands.

Collectible items are a way to reach brand-new audiences with your product. For instance, say you're a marketing leader at Axe and you're trying to get more young men to use your body spray.

You could make a four-pack of Axe with different sprays exclusive for Costco in a package that has a trading card of an emerging popular gamer like Clix or Bugha.* Collectors would realize that these are essentially the "rookie cards" of these individuals, and they'll go out and buy the body spray just for the rookie card.

Although they might be buying the product for the card, a high percentage would still use the body spray because now they have it, and if the product is good, a significant percentage of those people will continue to buy in the future. What you're able to do here is create "trial" of a new product but under the context of a cool, pop culture strategy that's different than, say, sampling an item at Costco.

I think collectibles are an enormous opportunity for brands, and I think we'll see more and more of them lean into it the same way they did in the 1950s, '60s, and '70s. It's a bigger genre than people think. It could take the form of trading cards, toys, even limited-edition collaborative sneakers.

---

* Full disclosure: VaynerSports represents both Clix and Bugha.

Brands can't just do billboards, print ads, and bad digital banner ads anymore. Lean heavily into social media and the other strategies I've talked about in this book, like event marketing, apparel and merchandise collaborations, mascots, and collectibles. This is the macro concept of day trading attention, aka marketing of the next decade.

CONCLUSION

CLOSING NOTES

The thesis of day trading attention is simple: Figure out where underpriced attention is and learn how to effectively storytell in those places. But as I always say, you can't just read about doing push-ups. Execution is the game, and that's the hard part. Brands, businesses, and influencers often find it difficult to keep up with all the latest platform changes happening constantly, and many of them ask me how to stay on top of it all. My honest answer? You've got to just set aside time and put in the work. With the TikTokification of social media, the opportunities today are much greater than ten years ago, but so is the effort required.

I thought if I wrote a detailed book that went deep on the strategies and tactics you need to know, it would serve as a manual that you can read and reread as you continue along your journey. As technology continues to advance, I believe the principles I talk about in this book will stay truer than ever. There are many exciting technologies I'm keeping tabs on in the AI and marketing landscape. We all know about tools like ChatGPT, but as AI grows in scale, we'll one day have the tools to analyze every important variable that goes into making a great piece of content. We'll be able to make hundreds, thousands, and tens of thousands of pieces of content per month with AI, put them out across platforms, and use technology to help us gather learnings to make the next piece of content better. We'll be able to execute the strategies in this book at an even greater scale, which makes it even more important to be a practitioner of the craft today.

I also believe AI is going to change consumer behavior in a massive way that will benefit those who invest in building brand. For instance, people today are having fun with ChatGPT by asking it to create comprehensive diet plans for people with various tastes or dietary restrictions. But imagine being able to say to your Alexa or Google Home voice device in the future: "My kids' friends are coming over between eight p.m. to ten p.m. Three of them are lactose intolerant, two like pizza, and one is vegan. Order some food delivery and have them leave it outside the door." People will use statements like these to do their shopping because it's easier than typing in "pizza near me" on Google and scrolling through the menu online. AI is going to eliminate friction in ways we can't even imagine today.

What does that mean for brands and businesses? If you're Starbucks, you wouldn't want a customer to say, "Send me a cold brew," to Alexa. You'd want him or her to say, "Send me a Starbucks cold brew." If people say, "Send me pizza" or "Book a massage appointment," then Amazon has the leverage in what pizza they

send, or where they book the massage. If large brands especially don't figure out how to build brand on underpriced attention channels, they're going to lose a ton of market share over the next few decades between AI and competing brands started by influencers.

The winners are going to be those who get curious about these modern advertising platforms and figure out how to storytell where there's underpriced attention. The losers, as always, will be those who sit on their hands or scoff at the new opportunities. Don't be like the people who laughed when I talked about the opportunities on Twitter in 2006, or when I decided to sell wine on the internet in 1996. Don't be like the small businesses who missed out on the underpriced nature of Google AdWords in the early 2000s, or everyone who gave up enormous organic reach potential on 2019 TikTok because their "customers weren't on it." All those people had to catch up later anyway. Today the game is all about taking advantage of the TikTokification of social media (which is still in its relatively early stages in 2024).

When something new comes along that's worth going all in on, you can bet that I'll be yelling about it. I'm always keeping a pulse on where consumer attention is shifting. Currently I'm looking into WhatsApp as a marketing channel, as well as playing with other channels like Pinterest, Threads, and even using AI to translate my voice into different languages. With the rise of blockchain technology, I'm looking out for decentralized social networks too and keeping an eye on consumer attention in virtual reality and the metaverse.

But day trading attention isn't about predicting "what's next." It's about staying on the pulse of where people's eyes and ears are today, and marketing for the "now," whenever that happens to be. I hope you put in the effort to truly become a practitioner of that, with this book as your guide.

ACKNOWLEDGMENTS

First, I want to thank my family, whom I love more than breathing.

Next, I want to thank Raghav Haran, my writer and collaborator for *Day Trading Attention* who also worked with me on my last book. Can't believe this is number two! I also want to thank the entire VaynerX team who helped in the process to make this book what it is, including McKenzie Dawkins, Siddharth Astir, Jon Morgenstern, Peter Chun, Marcus Krzastek, Hanna Park, Wanda Pogue, Rob Lenois, Brittney Diamond, Hugh Scallon, Jason Loomis, Nick Dio, Blaine Nicholls, Will Taylor, and everyone on Team GaryVee.

Finally, a huge thank-you to Hollis Heimbouch and everyone at Harper-Collins for always being great partners to work with.

NOTES

1. BigBoyTV, YouTube, 2020.
2. McCann, Modern Retail, 2022.
3. *USA Today*, 2023.
4. NPR, 2022.
5. Leichtman Research, 2023.
6. *AdAge*, 2022.
7. NBC Los Angeles, 2023.
8. TechCrunch, 2023.
9. Bloomberg, 2022.
10. TechCrunch, 2023.
11. Social Media Today, 2023.
12. Oxford Learner's Dictionaries, 2023.
13. Federal Reserve Bank of Minneapolis, 2023.
14. HUB Entertainment Research, 2023.
15. Business Insider, 2023.
16. Insider Intelligence, 2023.

BIBLIOGRAPHY

Barinka, Alex. "Meta's Instagram Users Reach 2 Billion, Closing in on Facebook (Meta)." Bloomberg.com, October 26, 2022. https://www.bloomberg.com/news/articles/2022-10-26/meta-s-instagram-users-reach-2-billion-closing-in-on-facebook.

BigBoyTV 2020. "Fleetwood Mac 'Dreams' TikTok Sensation Nathan Apodaca in the Big Interview." YouTube, October 6, 2020. Accessed September 28, 2023. https://youtu.be/BVCP8EJRaqU?si=eobYsRkco-nwMLbI.

Conti, Kristen. "A Look at How Much Super Bowl Commercials Cost in 2023, and through the Years." NBC Los Angeles, February 3, 2023. https://www.nbclosangeles.com/news/sports/super-bowl-commercials-how-much-do-they-cost-a-look-through-the-years/2822339/.

Herren, Parker. "TV Commercial Prices: Advertising Costs in the 2022–23 Season." *AdAge*, October 26, 2022. https://adage.com/article/media/tv-commercial-prices-advertising-costs-2022-23-season/2437106.

HUB Entertainment Research. "2023 Connected Home." Accessed October 9, 2023. https://hubresearchllc.com/reports/?category=2023&title=2023-connected-home.

Hutchinson, Andrew. "LinkedIn's Now Up to 930 Million Members, Continues to See Strong Engagement." Social Media Today, May 2, 2023. https://www.socialmediatoday.com/news/LinkedIn-Now-Up-to-930-Million-Members/649239/.

"Inflation Calculator." Federal Reserve Bank of Minneapolis. Accessed October 10, 2023. https://www.minneapolisfed.org/about-us/monetary-policy/inflation-calculator.

Konstantinovic, Daniel. "Almost Half of YouTube Viewership Happens on TV Screens." Insider Intelligence, May 8, 2023. https://www.insiderintelligence.com/content/almost-half-of-youtube-viewership-happens-on-tv-screens.

"Major Pay-TV Providers Lost about 5,900,000 Subscribers in 2022." Leichtman Research Group, March 3, 2023. https://leichtmanresearch.com/major-pay-tv-providers-lost-about-5900000-subscribers-in-2022/.

Mayer, Grace. "The Average TikTok User in the US Is an Adult 'Well Past College Age,' CEO Says." Business Insider. Accessed October 10, 2023. https://www.businessinsider.com/tiktok-user-average-age-united-states-adult-past-college-ceo-2023-3.

McCann, Maile. "'So Much of My Audience in One Place': The Rise of the TikTok Small Businesses." Modern Retail, May 4, 2022. Accessed September 28, 2023. https://www.modernretail.co/retailers/so-much-of-my-audience-in-one-place-the-rise-of-the-tiktok-small-businesses/.

Mehta, Ivan. "Google Says 2 Billion Logged in Monthly Users Are Watching YouTube Shorts." TechCrunch, July 26, 2023. https://techcrunch.com/2023/07/25/google-says-2-billion-logged-in-monthly-users-are-watching-youtube-shorts/

Myers, Amanda Lee. "Unlikely Book Hits No. 1 on Amazon after Daughter's TikTok Showed Dad's Toil, Low Sales." *USA Today*, February 20, 2023. https://www.usatoday.com/story/news/nation/2023/02/19/stone-maidens-book-bestseller-daughter-tiktok/11251731002/.

"Relevance Definition." Oxford Learner's Dictionaries. Accessed October 1, 2023. https://www.oxfordlearnersdictionaries.com/us/definition/english/relevance?q=relevance.

"Research Guides: American Women: Resources from the Moving Image Collections: Television." Television—American Women: Resources from the Moving Image Collections. Research Guides at Library of Congress. Accessed September 29, 2023. https://guides.loc.gov/american-women-moving-image/television.

Romo, Vanessa. "No Medals for 2022 Beijing Olympics. The Games Drew Their Lowest U.S. Ratings Ever." NPR, February 23, 2022. https://www.npr.org/2022/02/22/1082461546/no-medals-for-2022-beijing-olympics-the-games-drew-their-lowest-u-s-ratings-ever.

Silberling, Amanda. "Facebook Surpasses 3 Billion Monthly Active Users." TechCrunch, July 27, 2023. https://techcrunch.com/2023/07/26/facebook-3-billion-users/.

ABOUT THE AUTHOR

GARY VAYNERCHUK is the chairman of VaynerX, a modern-day communications holding company, and the active CEO of VaynerMedia, a contemporary global creative and media agency. He's also the creator of VeeFriends, a contemporary entertainment company that uses its unique art, compelling storytelling, and distinct collectibles to enhance its intellectual property. He is a *New York Times* bestselling author, a sought-after public speaker, and an early investor in companies like Facebook, X (Twitter), Tumblr, Venmo, Liquid Death, Coinbase, Slack, and Uber. He is a board/advisory member of Bojangles' Restaurants and Pencils of Promise, and a longtime Well Member of Charity: Water.

In his seventh business book, bestselling author, entrepreneur, and investor Gary Vaynerchuk offers fresh, in-depth advice to enhance brand development, grow sales, and beat the competition using modern advertising strategies grounded in social media.

IN his 2013 bestseller, *Jab, Jab, Jab, Right Hook*, Gary Vaynerchuk showed the world how to create winning content for underpriced attention channels. But since then, new platforms have emerged, others have become less relevant, and algorithms are incentivizing new styles of content. New skills are necessary to create advertising that builds brand and sales.

In his latest book, Vaynerchuk argues that today's fast-growing businesses, brands, content creators, and influencers have one thing in common: They've mastered storytelling in areas of underpriced attention, which predominantly exist across a handful of social media platforms. Informed by twenty-plus years of business and marketing success, Vaynerchuk contends that the biggest transformation and opportunity is the "TikTokification of Social Media." Increasingly, platforms are distributing content based on what users are interested in, rather than who they follow.

Small businesses, large corporations, and creators can take advantage of this trend to develop brand and grow sales by producing relevant, strategic content, even if they don't have an audience. But how does one make relevant content? What should advertisements look like in this new world?

In *Day Trading Attention*, Vaynerchuk provides detailed answers to these questions and more, revealing the tactics to master modern advertising with strategies you can apply to the moment you're currently living in.

GARY VAYNERCHUK is the chairman of VaynerX, a modern-day communications holding company, and the active CEO of VaynerMedia, a contemporary global creative and media agency. He's also the creator of VeeFriends, a contemporary entertainment company that uses its unique art, compelling storytelling, and distinct collectibles to enhance its intellectual property. He is a *New York Times* bestselling author, a sought-after public speaker, and an early investor in companies like Facebook, X (Twitter), Tumblr, Venmo, Liquid Death, Coinbase, Slack, and Uber. He is a board/advisory member of Bojangles' Restaurants and Pencils of Promise, and a longtime Well Member of Charity: Water.

HARPER
BUSINESS

An Imprint of HarperCollins*Publishers*

Cover design by Kyle Nguyen
Cover illustration by alex_skp/iStock Getty Images Plus via Getty Images
Author photograph by Team GaryVee

Discover great authors, exclusive offers, and more at hc.com.

Business & Economics

ISBN 978-0-06-339411-7

52199

9 780063 394117

EAN

USA $21.99

0524